# Rightly Dividing Romans Study Guide

## By Marianne Manley

## Acknowledgment

*To God be the glory for helping me write this book! I am grateful for the support of my dear husband Chuck and my children during this time. I would like to thank some of the many grace pastors who have helped me understand God's word rightly divided: Les Feldick, Richard Jordan, Tom Bruscha, Rick Jordan, David Reid, David O'Steen, Paul Lucas, and others. I was particularly helped by Shawn Brasseaux's informative articles on Forwhatsaithscriptures.org. I am delighted with the cover and artwork for the hymns by Madelein Wilkinson. I thank LeighAnn Mycko and others for their memes. I am grateful for Patty Carlson for proofreading and sign making. In preparing these books, I primarily read and study the word of God over and over again until the Holy Spirit helps me to understand His word better, but I also listen to sermons, read articles and books.*

**\*A note from the Author. After teaching on all Paul's letters and writing commentaries on them I am going through his letters again taking a closer look at each and every paragraph in conjunction with my more seasoned understanding. This is the new <u>closer walk series of the rightly dividing</u> of Paul's <u>mystery</u> letters from the rest of the Bible (<u>prophecy</u>). The goal is to help <u>accelerate the reader's spiritual growth and understanding of the Bible</u>. This study guide is meant to be <u>used along with the King James Bible</u>. Some important or difficult passages are quoted more completely and scrutinized more thoroughly. While Satan is preparing the world for antichrist, God's Spirit in us is working to prepare us to be useful sons here and in heaven. When some verses are found in Romans, I write (1:16) instead of (Rom. 1:16).**

**How to use this book: skim it first, read it using a ruler and a pen, when you find a great cross-reference or comment you can mark it in your Bible, circle and color important words, make notes so that you have them next time you read that passage. I recommend the Scofield Study Bible III in the King James Version. It is wise to get a leather cover for it that holds a pen and zips.**

**I recommend reading <u>*God's Secret A Primer with Pictures for How to Rightly Divide the Word of Truth*</u> before this book. For a more complete between-the-Bible-text analysis please read our commentaries on all of Paul's letters, Acts and Hebrews. We have a salvation booklet. All glory to our Lord Jesus Christ!**

# Table of Content

## Foreword

"Just a closer walk with Thee, Grant it, Jesus, is my plea, Daily walking close to Thee, Let it be, dear Lord, let it be" (from the hymn *Just a Closer Walk with Thee* author unknown, 1940). How do we have a closer walk with God? By examining His every word more closely again and again. We have to compare verses with verses and recognize their dispensational setting.

The Bible cannot be understood unless it is rightly divided (2 Timothy 2:15). We are not to divide among or between Paul's letters, but we are to divide the Bible where God divides it, between Paul's letters and the rest of the Bible. Romans to Philemon are one unit of information for us written to Christ's group that will live "eternal in the heavens" (2 Cor. 5:1), while the rest of the Bible is for the believers who will live on earth.

We divide Paul's letters <u>from</u> Genesis to John and Hebrews to Revelation with Acts being a transition book. We divide between Christ's earthly ministry to Israel through Peter and the eleven (Matt. 10:1-7; Gal. 2:7-9) to Christ's ministry to His heavenly group through Paul (Acts 26:16-18; Rom. 11:13).

Paul told the Philippians that they helped him financially "from the beginning of the gospel" (Phil. 4:15). This means since he founded that church in Philippi in Acts 16 on his second apostolic journey until he wrote to them from Rome which joins Paul's Acts ministry with his prison epistles. Again, <u>God does not divide among or between Paul's letters, and neither should we.</u>

All scripture is "for us" but not all scripture is written "to us" or "about us," most of the Bible is written to and about the nation of Israel. But all of the Bible is "for our learning" (Rom. 15:4). We are to "Put on the whole armour of God, that ye may be able to stand against the wiles of the devil" (Eph. 6:11). <u>We defeat Satan's false doctrine, by understanding ALL of the Bible rightly divided.</u> But of course, we should pay special attention to Paul's 13 letters since Paul is the apostle of the Gentiles (Rom. 11:13) and he wrote to all of us who are living in the dispensation of grace, even the Jews.

Why is Romans such an important book to understand? Romans is a masterpiece, our handbook for Christian living. It is the <u>foundational basic teaching for the body of Christ,</u> which needs to be mastered before we are ready to move on to the advanced doctrine in Ephesians. Romans, written during Acts, is not the first book Paul wrote, but it is first doctrinally.

# Just a Closer Walk with Thee
Author unknown (1940)

I am weak, but Thou art strong;
Jesus, keep me from all wrong;
I'll be satisfied as long
As I walk, let me walk close to Thee.

*Refrain:*
Just a closer walk with Thee,
Grant it, Jesus, is my plea,
Daily walking close to Thee,
Let it be, dear Lord, let it be.

Through this world of toil and snares,
If I falter, Lord, who cares?
Who with me my burden shares?
None but Thee, dear Lord, none but Thee.

When my feeble life is o'er,
Time for me will be no more;
Guide me gently, safely o'er
To Thy kingdom shore, to Thy shore.

# Introduction to ROMANS

**The theme of Romans is the righteousness of God. Romans explains how God solved the sin problem. Romans tells us what Jesus accomplished by the cross. No one can go to heaven without the imputed righteousness of Jesus Christ.**

**The PROBLEM: God is holy and nothing unholy can come before Him without being obliterated. The oldest book in the Bible stated the problem. "How should man be just with God? (Job 9:2) We inherited the sin nature from Adam (Rom. 5:12).**

**The SOLUTION: Jesus Christ paid the price for our sin with His own blood. He died the death we deserved, and then the sinless Son of God rose from the dead. We are saved when we believe the good news God gave to Paul. "I declare unto you the gospel . . . By which also ye are saved . . . how that Christ died for our sins . . . was buried, and . . . rose again the third day according to the scriptures" (1 Cor. 15:3, 4). When the Father sees our faith resting in His Son's blood payment on the cross and His resurrection then He declares us justified. Jesus took our sins on the cross and when we believe we receive His righteousness credited to our account or imputed. This is incredible! What good news! What a great deal! Romans chapter four explains imputation.**

**IMPUTATION**

CHRIST'S RIGHTEOUSNESS

OUR SINS

"For he hath made him to be sin for us, who knew no sin; that we might be made the righteousness of God in him."
2 CORINTHIANS 5:21 KJB

"For what saith the scripture? Abraham believed God, and it was counted unto him for righteousness."
ROMANS 4:3 KJB

"But for us also, to whom it shall be imputed, if we believe on him that raised up Jesus our Lord from the dead; Who was delivered for our offences, and was raised again for our justification."
ROMANS 4:24-25 KJB

**If we have received His imputed righteousness, what else do we need? The answer is nothing. We are totally and completely forgiven.**

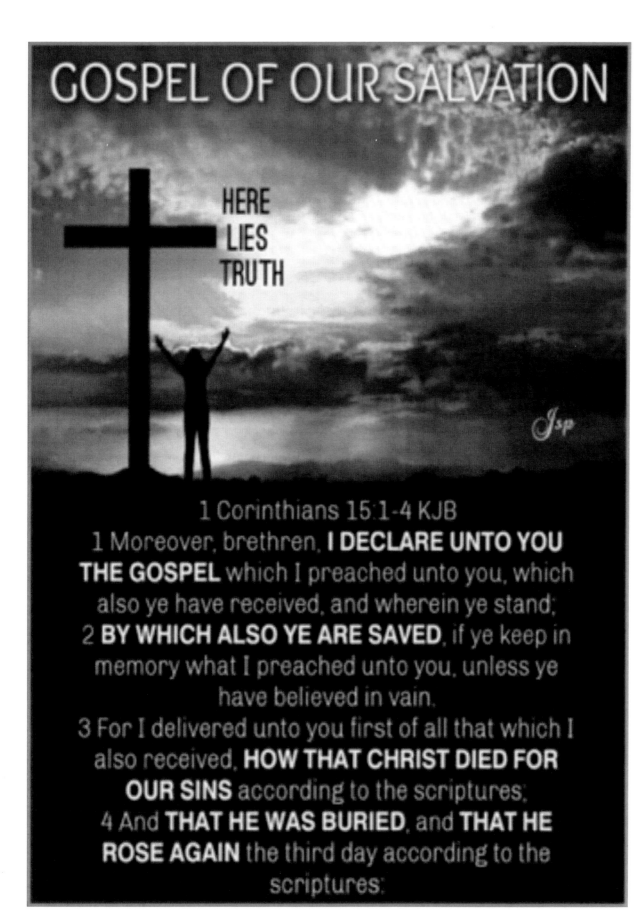

GOSPEL OF OUR SALVATION

HERE
LIES
TRUTH

1 Corinthians 15:1-4 KJB

1 Moreover, brethren, **I DECLARE UNTO YOU THE GOSPEL** which I preached unto you, which also ye have received, and wherein ye stand;

2 **BY WHICH ALSO YE ARE SAVED**, if ye keep in memory what I preached unto you, unless ye have believed in vain.

3 For I delivered unto you first of all that which I also received, **HOW THAT CHRIST DIED FOR OUR SINS** according to the scriptures;

4 And **THAT HE WAS BURIED**, and **THAT HE ROSE AGAIN** the third day according to the scriptures:

**Justification Summary**
The sinner that believes is justified because Christ "who knew no sin," bore our sin on the cross, being made "sin for <u>us</u> . . . that <u>we</u> might be made the righteousness of God in him" (2 Cor. 5:21).
(1) Justification is an act of declaring a person righteous (when we believe the glorious gospel and for Israel under the New Covenant in the kingdom).
(2) It is by God's grace (Rom. 3:24, Titus 3:4, 5).
(3) Both the Gentiles and the Jews failed repeatedly and God proved that all believers in heaven and earth need His Son's righteousness (Rom. 3:21-26).
(4) It is by faith alone, not works (Rom. 4:5, 14).
(5) It is the judicial act of God where He justly declares and treats as righteous the one who has received the imputed righteousness of Jesus Christ by faith. The judge Himself has declared that nothing is laid to his charge. Having the imputed righteousness of Christ, we have total forgiveness (Rom. 4:3, 23-25; 8:1, 31-34).

**The Three Rights**
**(1) Right gospel (1 Cor. 15:3, 4)**
**(2) Right Bible (King James Bible)**
**(3) Right doctrine for the body of Christ (Romans to Philemon).**

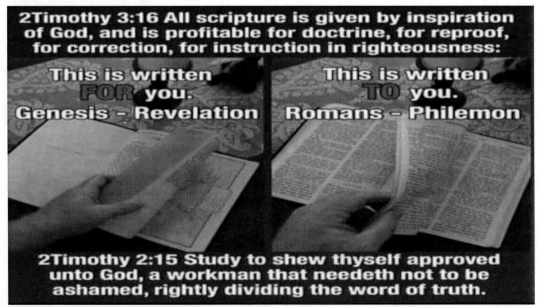

After we are saved, God wants us to know Him, serve Him as sons, and gain rewards in heaven. We can only be effective if we "Study to shew thyself approved unto God, a workman that needeth not to be ashamed, rightly dividing the word of truth" (2 Tim. 2:15). <u>We divide the Bible where God divides it.</u> All the Bible is "for us," but Romans to Philemon is written "to us." Jesus Christ's doctrine to us through Paul produces godliness in us which is <u>profitable in this life and in the life to come</u> (1 Tim. 4:8, 6:3).

# ROMANS IN A NUTSHELL

Paul wrote to the believers in Rome, the capital of the Roman Empire, from Corinth c. AD 58, after having been the "apostle of the Gentiles" (11:13) <u>for about twenty-three years.</u> Paul wants to edify them with more truth.

Chapters 1-5 The book of Romans systematically and logically explains how the righteous God can justify (declare righteous) an unrighteous sinner by faith (alone). <u>All the world is guilty before God</u> (Rom. 1-3:20). In Adam all sin (5:12). <u>Christ was crucified for our sins and rose again</u> for our justification (Rom. 3:21-5:21). Not only was Christ crucified and rose for us, but <u>believers are spiritually crucified and risen with Christ</u> (Chapters 6-8). Who we were in Adam has been spiritually crucified (Rom. 6:3, 4), and now we can have Christ's life in us. We can serve God as we <u>know, reckon, and yield</u> to the fact that we are <u>"dead indeed unto sin, but alive unto God through Jesus Christ our Lord"</u> (Rom. 6:11). We still have the sinful flesh residing in our mortal bodies which is activated by the law of Moses. His purpose is that we "be conformed to the image of his Son" (Rom. 8:29) by His doctrine. God has now elected (chosen) to show mercy to the Gentiles (8:33). (Chapters 9-11) Paul tells believers in the body of Christ that God was righteous to set Israel aside temporarily and begin the dispensation of grace to save Gentiles. The unbelieving Gentiles and Jews are His <u>vessels of wrath.</u> The believing remnant of Israel (Peter's group still present but on hold at the time of the writing of Romans) and the believing Gentiles are His <u>vessels of mercy</u> (11:5, 23, 24). <u>Through Israel's fall salvation is come unto the Gentiles</u> (11:11, 12). <u>God is able to dispense grace to the world because of the cross of Christ, and He will save any sinner who believes what His Son has done until the Rapture.</u> But, after the "fullness of the Gentiles be come in" God will resume His dealings with Israel (11:25-27). (Chapters 12-16) Practical instructions on how to live unto God. It is reasonable for us to serve God. After we have been educated by God's word, <u>we offer our bodies a living sacrifice for Christ to live His life through us</u> (12:1, 2). We serve God acceptably as we live by faith in the word of God rightly divided. <u>As sons of God, our motivation is love and gratitude to God.</u> Paul concludes the letter with a benediction: Believers are stabilized by three things: (1) Paul's <u>"my gospel"</u> which is justification by faith, (2) "and <u>the preaching of Jesus Christ, according to the revelation of the mystery,</u> which was <u>kept secret since the world began"</u> (Romans to Philemon), (3) "and by the <u>scriptures of the prophets,"</u> (the <u>prophecy</u> in the rest of the Bible) (16:25-27). All nations are commanded by the everlasting God to believe the entire Bible (the whole counsel of God) rightly divided (2 Timothy 2:15).

# Why is Romans the First Book of Paul's Letters in the Bible?

Although Romans was the sixth book Paul wrote, it is first in God's order of scripture because it is the foundational doctrine for the body of Christ. It was written from Corinth (Acts 20:3) during his three months stay there after the <u>uproar</u> in Ephesus, before Paul left to bring a contribution to the poor Messianic kingdom saints in Jerusalem. Paul shared the information he learned in Ephesus and <u>most likely just finished teaching Romans at Corinth</u>.

The 13 letters of Paul follow the order given in 2 Tim. 3:16: <u>All scripture is given by inspiration of God</u>, and is profitable for <u>DOCTRINE</u>, for <u>REPROOF</u>, for <u>CORRECTION</u>, for <u>INSTRUCTION IN RIGHTEOUSNESS</u> (practical living).

Romans = doctrine
1 & 2 Corinthians = reproof
Galatians = correction
Ephesians = doctrine
Philippians = reproof
Colossians = correction
1 & 2 Thessalonians = doctrine, instruction in righteousness
1 & 2 Timothy, Titus, Philemon = doctrine, instruction in righteousness

Romans (foundational doctrine), 1 & 2 Corinthian (reproof for not living according to the doctrine in Romans), and Galatians (correction for leaving grace and living under the law). Paul was put on house arrest in the last chapter of Acts, Acts 28. These epistles were written before Paul received the full revelation of the <u>mystery</u>. They focus on foundational doctrines and are best understood when read together.

The order of Paul's Acts epistles including when and where were written:

| Galatians | 1 Thess. | 2 Thess. | 1 Cor. | 2 Cor. | Romans |
|---|---|---|---|---|---|
| Acts 15:35 | Acts 18:5 | Acts 18:11 | Acts 19:10 | Acts 20:1 | Acts 20:3 |
| Antioch | Corinth | Corinth | Ephesus | Macedonia | Corinth |
| AD 52* | AD 53 | AD 53 | AD 56 | AD 57 | AD 58 |

*approximate dates

The order of Paul's post Acts epistles when and where they were written:

| Eph. | Col. | Philemon | Phil. | 1 Tim. | Titus | 2 Tim. |
|---|---|---|---|---|---|---|
| Rome | Rome | Rome | Rome | Macedonia | Macedonia | Rome |
| AD 63 | AD 63 | AD 63 | AD 63 | AD 65 | AD 65 | AD 67 |

*Galatians 2:7 (KJV):*

**"But contrariwise, when they saw that the <u>gospel of the uncircumcision</u> was committed unto me, as the <u>gospel of the circumcision</u> was unto Peter;" ~PAUL**

I don't know why when people read that verse they cannot see TWO distinct gospels. It says it right there in black and white and has been sitting there for hundreds of years: The gospel of the Circumcision was unto PETER! The gospel of the Uncircumcision was unto ME (Paul)!

# Comparison Chart of Christ's Earthly and Heavenly Ministry

| Peter and Christ's Earthly Ministry | Paul and Christ's Heavenly Ministry |
|---|---|
| Prophecy regarding the kingdom on earth. | Mystery regarding His heavenly kingdom. |
| Preached what the prophets had SPOKEN . . . SINCE THE WORLD BEGAN (Acts 3:21). | Preached the mystery KEPT SECRET SINCE THE WORLD BEGAN (Rom. 16:25). |
| Given info from Christ on earth (Rom. 15:8). | Given info from Christ in heaven (Gal. 1:12). |
| Head of the 12 apostles to the 12 tribes (Matt. 16:19) | Christ's one apostle to the one body of Christ (Rom. 11:13). |
| Gospel of the circumcision (Gal. 2:7) was to the believing remnant of Israel, the little flock (Luke 12:32) which is Peter's group. | Gospel of the uncircumcision (Gal. 2:7-9) heathen (all unsaved Jews and Gentiles) |
| "These twelve Jesus sent forth, and commanded them, saying, Go not into the way of the Gentiles, and into any city of the Samaritans enter ye not: But go rather to the lost sheep of the house of Israel" (Matt. 10:5, 6). "Lord, wilt thou at this time restore again the kingdom to Israel? (Acts 1:6) | "I have appeared unto thee [Paul] for this purpose, to make thee a minister and a witness both of these things which thou hast seen, and of those things in the which I will appear unto thee; Delivering thee from the people [Jews], and from the Gentiles, unto whom now I send thee" (Acts 26:16, 17). |
| Paul was not one of the 12 (1 Cor. 15:5-8). Matthias was (Acts 1:26). | Paul was first one saved (placed) into the body of Christ (1 Tim. 1:15, 16). |
| Hope of resurrection in the kingdom on earth to sit on one of the 12 thrones (Matt. 19:28). | Hope of being "caught up" (1 Thess. 4:16, 17) and live "eternal in the heavens" (2 Cor. 5:1) |
| Israel was to be a "kingdom of priests" (Ex. 19:5, 6) a royal priesthood (1 Peter 2:9). | Paul said, "we are ambassadors for Christ" (2 Cor. 5:20) and peculiar people (Titus 2:14). |
| Message. Preached the gospel of the kingdom Jesus Christ is the Son of God to sit on the throne of David (Matt. 9:35, Mk 1:14, 15). | Preached the gospel of Christ, justification by faith in Christ's death for our sins on the cross, burial, and resurrection (1 Cor. 15:3, 4). |
| Israel's national salvation (atonement) will be at Christ's Second Coming to earth (1 Peter 1:5-7, 13) | Paul said the members of the body of Christ "have now received atonement" the instant they believe (Rom. 5:11). |
| Israel is to rise and shine and save Gentiles in prophecy. "Arise, shine . . . and the Gentiles shall come to thy light" (Isa. 60:1-3). | "I say then, . . . through their fall [the nation of Israel] salvation is come unto the Gentiles" (Rom. 11:12) in mystery. |
| Christ was a minister of the circumcision [believing remnant of Israel] (Rom. 15:8). | Paul was blinded by the glory of the ascended risen glorified Lord Jesus Christ (Acts 22:11) |
| Peter preached water baptism, "repent and be baptized" (Acts 2:38). | Paul said, "For Christ sent me not to baptize, but to preach the gospel" (1 Cor. 1:17). |
| Jesus said, "I am not sent but unto the lost sheep of the house of Israel" (Matt. 15:24). | Paul said, "made known to all nations for the obedience of faith" (Rom. 16:26). |
| ". . . she shall bring forth a son, and thou shalt call his name JESUS: for he shall save his people [Jews] from their sins" (Matt. 1:21). | From now on we no longer know Christ according to His earthly ministry "henceforth know we him no more"(2 Cor. 5:16). |
| Jesus came to earth "to give his life a ransom for many [believing Israel]" (Matt. 20:28). | "Who gave himself a ransom for all, to be testified in due time" (1 Tim. 2:6). |

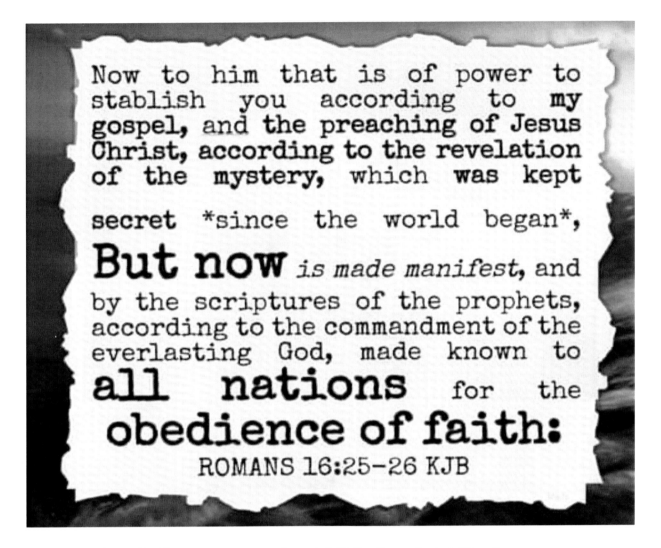

Now to him that is of power to stablish you according to my gospel, and the preaching of Jesus Christ, according to the revelation of the mystery, which was kept

secret *since the world began*,

But now is made manifest, and by the scriptures of the prophets, according to the commandment of the everlasting God, made known to all nations for the obedience of faith:

ROMANS 16:25-26 KJB

Paul says how believers are saved, established, and stabilized:

"Now to him that is of power to stablish you

(1) according to <u>my gospel</u>, [which Christ from heaven gave to Paul, the imputed righteousness of Christ by faith in the gospel (1 Cor. 15:3, 4; 2 Cor. 5:21).]

(2) and <u>the preaching of Jesus Christ, according to the revelation of the MYSTERY</u>, which was <u>kept secret since the world began</u>, <u>But now is made manifest</u>, [but now is made known Christ's ministry from heaven to us through Paul (Romans to Philemon).]

(3) and <u>by the scriptures of the prophets</u>, according to the commandment of the everlasting God, made known to <u>all nations</u> for the obedience of faith" (Rom. 16:25, 26). [prophecy in the rest of the Bible from a Pauline point of view. All nations are to be established by these three things in the dispensation of grace.]

**Does it Matter Which Bible I Use?**

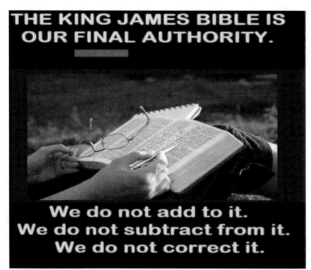

Yes, absolutely. Here is an example. The King James Bible says, "For I am not ashamed of the gospel <u>of Christ</u>: for it is the power of God unto salvation to every one that believeth; to the Jew first, and also to the Greek" (Rom. 1:16). The New International Version (NIV) just says "the gospel" <u>leaving out "of Christ"</u> and so does the NASB and the ESV and the RSV. The Amplified Bible has *of Christ* in italics and the NKJV has a foot note that says that "NU-Text omits *of Christ* (Westcott and Hort omitted it in their false Greek New Testament which is the basic text for most modern versions.)

The King James translators italicized words which they included for clarity but were not in the original manuscripts. Here is an example "I am *he*" (John 8:28). This lets the reader see at a glance what is written in the original word of God. The originals have turned to dust a long time ago. God preserved His word through a multiplicity of copies as He said He would in Psalms 12:6, 7. *Please note that in the King James Version "of Christ" were not put in italics because those words were in the majority of manuscripts. There are no errors in the King James Bible therefore it is best to use it in our Bible study.

Remember:
It is not enough to own a Bible; you need a King James Bible.
It is not enough to read a King James Bible; you need to study it.
It is not enough to study a King James Bible; you need to right divide it.
It is not enough the rightly divide a King James Bible; you need to believe it.
It is not enough to believe a King James Bible; you need to teach it.
It is not enough to teach a King James Bible; you need to guard it.
It is not enough to guard a King James Bible; you need to never let it go!

**God's Timeline**
**The order of the books in the Bible reveals the order of events in the world.**

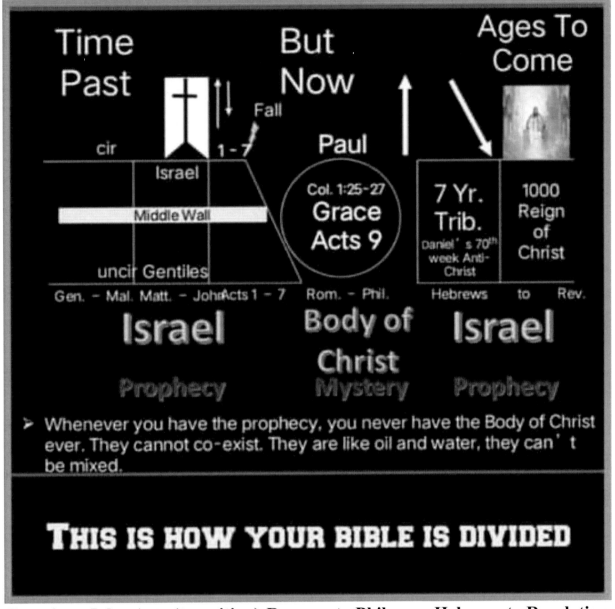

Genesis to John-Acts (transition)-Romans to Philemon-Hebrews to Revelation

<u>What is the mystery</u>? The mystery (Eph. 3:1-9) is that God is saving another group of people, the body of Christ, during Israel's national blindness (the dispensation of grace) to live "eternal in the heavens" (2 Cor. 5:1). We are living in an <u>un-prophesied parenthetical period of time</u>, the dispensation of grace, which is flanked by two appearings of Christ: the appearing of the risen glorified Lord Jesus Christ to our apostle Paul (Rom. 11:13) in Acts 9, and His imminent appearing to Rapture the body of Christ. After our Rapture, Christ will resume His dealings with Israel (Rom. 11:25-27).

# The Four Foundational Cornerstones of Romans

**1. JUSTIFICATION** (Chapters 1-5) Justified by faith in Christ's death for our sins, burial, and resurrection; believers receive His imputed righteousness.

**2. SANCTIFICATION** (Chapters 6-8) Our old man (who we were in Adam) was crucified with Christ and we were raised in newness of His life and can serve Him.

**3. DISPENSATIONAL** (Chapters 9-11) God has now elected that the Gentiles (all nations) can be saved. (9) Like a potter, God can make of the same lump (Israel) a vessel of honor (a nation of the believing remnant) and a vessel of dishonor (unbelieving Israel). God elected to show mercy to His vessels of mercy the believing remnant of Israel (now on hold) and the Gentiles in this dispensation, while apostate Israel was a vessel of wrath. (10). Paul says Israel was ignorant of the perfect righteousness of God and thought they could keep the law and establish their own righteousness. But Jews may be saved at present by believing the "word of faith, which <u>we preach</u>." God will save (from eternal hellfire) any Jew or Gentile and give them Christ's righteousness if they believe in their heart that God raised the Lord Jesus from the dead. Israel heard the gospel that Peter's group preached but refused to believe. (11) Has God cast away His people? No, because Paul was saved and he was a Jew. <u>God saved a remnant of Israel (Peter's group) and the rest were blinded</u>. The apostate nation of Israel stumbled at the cross, then fell in Acts 7 (from being above to the same level as the Gentile nations). Through their <u>fall</u> salvation has gone to the Gentiles. Paul speaks to the <u>Gentiles</u> as their apostle and says <u>they are a wild olive tree</u> that has been grafted into the good olive tree (11:13, 17). We are living during the dispensation of grace, Israel's national blindness, which ends at the Rapture with fullness of the Gentiles (11:25). Israel's future hope has been delayed (11:26-29). In His wisdom, God's present purpose is to conclude all in unbelief so He can have mercy on all (11:30-36).

**4. PRACTICAL APPLICATION** (Chapters 12-16) Christ teaches us through Paul how we are to live as sons of God as a result of what was taught in chapters 1-11. We offer our bodies a living sacrifice for Christ to live through (12:1-2). Our service to the believers (12:3-16). Our service to the unbelievers (12:17-21). Our service under government created by God for the purpose of law and order (13:1-7). Our service to all men. We are to love others as ourselves (13:8-14). Our service to the weaker believers (14:1-23). Concluding information. Be of <u>one mind</u> and <u>one mouth</u> behind apostle Paul glorifying God the Father. Christ's past ministry was to the circumcision with the intent of saving the Gentiles in prophecy (15:8-12), Paul's present ministry (15:13-33). Paul's salutations (16:1-16), Paul's warning (16:17-20). Tertius says hello (16:21-24). Paul's Benediction (16:25-27).

| JUSTIFICATION 1-5 | SANCTIFICATION 6-8 |
|---|---|
| Position. The Father can remain just, and declare a believer in Christ justified who has received His Son's <u>imputed righteousness</u> by faith in His blood payment for our sins on the cross and resurrection. Our <u>position</u> in Christ is perfect, but spiritual growth helps to make our state match our standing. | State. Set apart for service. Baptized (our spiritual identification) with Christ's death, burial, and resurrection. Dead to sin, dead to the law, alive unto God by His Spirit in us, for the purpose of being fully functioning sons of God conformed <u>by the doctrine</u> to the image of His Son and joint heirs with Christ. |
| DISPENSATIONAL 9-11 | APPLICATION 12-16 |
| Was God righteous to set Israel aside? By Israel's fall salvation has gone to the Gentiles, does that mean that God has cast away His people Israel? Paul delivers to us Christ's teaching on the dispensational change which involves nations. Israel's national stumbling, fall, temporary spiritual blindness in part, her future hope, and God's present purpose to save the Gentiles. | Application of the doctrine. Our walk as sons. Our service to God, service to the body, service to the lost, service under human government, service in the world, and service to weaker brethren. Christ's ministry to Israel in the past for the purpose of saving the Gentiles in prophecy. Paul's present ministry, his friends in Rome, his warning, and concluding revelation. |

**\*Each Cornerstone is connected to the others and makes up the entire letter.**

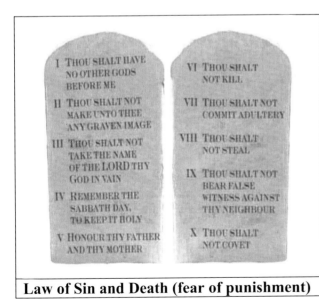

| Law of Sin and Death (fear of punishment) | Law of the Spirit of life in Christ Jesus |
|---|---|

**Romans Outline**
Written from Corinth (Acts 20:2, 3) c. AD 58.
**Theme:** The gospel of Christ reveals "the righteousness of God" (1:16, 17, 3:22)
**Key verses:** "For I am not ashamed of the gospel of Christ: for it is the power of God unto salvation to every one that believeth; to the Jew first, and also to the Greek. For therein is the righteousness of God revealed from faith to faith: as it is written, The just shall live by faith" (Rom. 1:16, 17)
**Purpose:** To establish saints in "the faith" (Rom. 1:11, 6:17, 16:25)
**Greetings** (1:1-7) and **purpose statement** (1:8-17)

**I. Sin (Righteousness needed)**
A. Gentiles under sin (1:18-32)
B. Jews under sin (2:1-3:8)
C. Whole world under sin (3:9-20)

**II. Salvation (Righteousness imputed)**
A. Justification explained (3:21-31)
B. Imputation explained using Abraham (4)
C. Result of justification (5)

**III. Sanctification (Righteousness imparted for service)**
A. Our new identity in Christ (6)
B. Our new problem in the flesh (7)
C. Our new power in the Spirit (8)

**IV. Was God righteous to set Israel aside? (Righteousness Rejected)**
A. God's election of the Gentiles and rejection of Israel (9)
B. Present salvation opportunity for individual Jews (10)
C. Has God cast away His people? (11)

**V. Serving God Out of Love and Gratitude (Righteousness practiced)**
A. How do we live a life of service to God? (12)
B. Living with government (13)
C. The weaker brother and debatable things (14)
D. Paul's Ministry to the Gentiles (15)
E. Christ was a minister to the Jews with Gentiles in mind in prophecy (15:8-12)
F. Paul talks of his apostleship and the ministry God sent him to do (15:13-33)

**VI. Conclusion**
A. Salutations to friends. Benediction concerning the revelation of the mystery (16)

**Romans Chapter Review Sentences**

1. The power of the gospel of Christ, His righteousness. Gentiles are under sin.

2. The Jews who had the law and did not believe in Jesus Christ are under sin.

3. The whole world is guilty before God, but God has solved the sin problem and saved believers in time past and in the present dispensation of grace.

4. We receive Christ's imputed righteousness when we believe what He did.

5. The result of justification is peace and access to God. We have much more in Christ who died for us, than we lost in Adam. His righteousness totally rids our sin.

6. We are dead to sin, but alive unto God. How shall we then live?

7. We are dead to the law, which activates our sinful flesh. Good to know.

8. The doctrine allows us to walk not after the flesh, but after the Spirit.

9. Paul explains that God has elected to show mercy to the Gentiles.

10. Why Israel fell and the Jews present salvation opportunity. Today, individual Jews can be saved by believing the gospel Paul preached.

11. Paul explains Israel's blindness in part during this dispensation. God will still keep His promises to the nation of Israel after Gentile believers are Raptured.

12. We are to present our bodies a living sacrifice for Christ to live through, and to be transformed into the image of His Son, by renewing our minds.

13. We can be model citizens and when we "love thy neighbor as thy self." God has set up governmental structures to protect us.

14. Help the weak in Pauline doctrine to be strong. Do not judge others concerning minor issues. God knows the motives of our heart and He will judge.

15. Christ has sent Paul to directly be the minister to the Gentiles.

16. Greetings, warning, and Benediction.

**Romans Chapter 1 Gentiles under sin**

**Romans is the crucial foundational doctrine for the dispensation of grace and is the most important book in the Bible for all to study and understand. As we begin to read and believe the Bible, His Spirit in us helps us to understand more. In Romans, Paul addresses the believing Gentiles but sometimes he identifies himself with the Jews and at other times with the body of Christ. Paul speaks of the present dispensational shift in several passages (1:1-11, 3:21-31, chapters 9-11, 13:11-14, 15:7-16, 16:25-27). Gentiles means nations.**

**1:1-7 "Paul, a servant of Jesus Christ, called to be an apostle, separated unto the gospel of God, (Which he had promised afore by his prophets in the holy scriptures,)"** (1:1). God called Paul to be an apostle, he was separate from the twelve apostles. As God's spokesman, Paul writes to the believers in the body of Christ in Rome but also speaks about the unsaved Jews and Gentiles and the first saved Jewish remnant. Jesus Christ, of the seed of David, was promised in the prophetic scriptures. Paul, who saw the ascended, risen, glorified Lord Jesus Christ on the road to Damascus and was blinded by His light, confirms that Christ was **"declared to the Son of God with power, according to the spirit of holiness, by the resurrection from the dead"** (1:4). Paul's ministry is to all nations. **"By whom** [the Son] **we have received grace and apostleship, for obedience to the faith among all nations, for his name"** (1:5). The Romans are among the Gentile nations who were also called by Christ when they heard and believed the gospel. He salutes them from God our Father and the Lord Jesus Christ. God is able to dispense grace and peace to the world because of the cross of Christ (2 Cor. 5:19).

**1:8-17** Their mutual faith is spoken of throughout the world (1:8, 12). Paul longs to communicate the further revelation of the mystery that Christ has given Him to the believers at Rome. Paul thanks God for them and prays that it will be His will for him to visit them after he has delivered a monetary gift to the poor Messianic kingdom saints in Jerusalem (15:24-28). He has been too busy ministering to visit and hopes they have been doing the same. But now he is ready to preach the gospel (justification by faith) to them also. Paul is not ashamed, he knows that the gospel of Christ **"is the power of God unto salvation to every one that believeth; to the Jew first, and also to the Greek. For therein is the righteousness of God revealed from faith to faith: as it is written, The just shall live by faith"** (1:16, 17). God revealed the need for His righteousness (Phil. 3:9). Our faith rests in what the Son did by His faith. We receive the righteousness Christ had by His perfect faith when we believe what He did. The power of God translates us out of Adam into Christ and justified us. We live by faith in what God said rightly divided.

**1:18-23** Paul just finished speaking of the <u>righteousness of God and now contrasts</u> <u>the unrighteousness of the heathen</u>. Because God is righteous, He has <u>wrath against</u> <u>all ungodly, unrighteous unbelievers</u> who hold the truth in unrighteousness. <u>How</u> <u>did the heathen become the heathen</u>? They rejected God. They are <u>without excuse</u> because God has revealed Himself to them since the creation of the world. (His revelation in creation is enough to know about God, but not enough to know Him personally, for this we need to read and study His word.) <u>God progressively gave</u> <u>the Gentiles up and over to their evil ways beginning at the tower of Babel</u> (Genesis 10 and 11) because when they knew God they did not worship Him. "**Because that, when they knew God, they glorified him not as God**, **neither** **were thankful; but became vain in their imaginations, and their foolish heart** **was darkened. Professing themselves to be wise, they became fools, And** **changed the glory of the uncorruptible God into an image made like to** **corruptible man, and to birds, and fourfooted beasts, and creeping things**" (1:21-23). They changed the glory of God and made idols (notice the devolution from men, to four-footed beasts, to creeping things). <u>Unbelievers are under the</u> <u>wrath of God</u> and the high standard of the law, but not the saved (1 Tim. 1:9).

**1:24-32** "**Who changed the truth of God into <u>a lie</u>, and <u>worshipped and served</u>** **<u>the creature more than the Creator</u>, who is blessed for ever. Amen**" (1:25). The Gentiles were under Satan's power (Acts 26:18). The ultimate <u>lie</u> will be Satan incarnate in Antichrist claiming to be Christ. After they rejected God for idols, God gave the Gentiles up to the unclean lust of their own hearts. <u>From adultery to same-</u> <u>sex relations and then to a reprobate mind</u>. They were not thankful or thinking about God. <u>Israel was the "covenant breakers" (1:31) they broke their covenant</u> <u>with God when they made a golden calf at the foot of Mount Sinai (Ex. 19:8, 24:7,</u> <u>32: 4, 8)</u>. The more they degraded God in their minds the more they lived degraded perverted lives. The world has gone rapidly downhill during our own lifetime. <u>A</u> <u>reprobate mind is lacking His Spirit</u>. They received the reward that was fitting for their dark evil deeds and minds. Paul gives a whole list of their sinful acts. They know that God will hold them accountable and that they are worthy of eternal death but they still continue in their sin and take pleasure in following sinners.

**Romans Chapter 2 Jews under sin**

**2:1-16** The Jews are also inexcusable because they broke their covenant with God and they do the same evil things that they accuse the Gentiles of doing. Paul does not come right out and say that he is speaking about the Jews right away, he gradually reveals that he is addressing the Jews, so they will not be offended and will keep reading. "Give none offence, neither to the Jews [unsaved], nor to the Gentiles [unsaved], nor to the church of God [the body of Christ]" (1 Cor. 10:30). God's wrath is not only against the idolatry and sensuality of the Gentiles, but against the hypocritical self-superiority of religious pretense and abuse of spiritual privilege. Everyone who is unsaved is under God's wrath, including the Jews. "But we [Jews]" (2:2) are sure that God will judge right. Do you think you will escape the judgment of God? (2:3). God has been patient toward you. God would grant eternal life to those who keep the law perfectly, but no human could (3:10, 23). God is fair, loving, and gentle. It is His rich goodness and forbearance and longsuffering that leads all mankind to change their mind about who He is and what He has done (2:4). You are hardening your impenitent (not willing to repent) heart and refusing to believe God and are adding to the crimes that you will be judged for at the GWTJ (2:5). God will judge every man according to what he has done. If you have never sinned, you will receive eternal life (2:7). But wrath to the disobedient unbelievers. Paul mentions the Jews by name in 2:9. All sinners will perish, those who sin with the law, and those who sin without it. God is not a respecter of persons; He does not care if you are a Jew or a Gentile unbeliever (2:11). Those who did not have the law will perish and those who had the law will be judged by it. Jews have to do what the law said, not just hear it (2:13). When the Gentiles naturally obey the law they show that they have the law written in their heart and their conscience is a witness either accusing or excusing them. Paul said that Jesus Christ will judge the secrets of men at the Great White Throne Judgment according to "my gospel." They will be judged by whether or not they are justified having received the righteousness of Christ (His life, His Spirit) by faith in what God told them to believe (2:16; GWTJ Rev. 20:11-15). Paul says "my gospel" (2:16) to differentiate his gospel from the gospel of the twelve.

**2:17-29** "**Behold, thou art called a Jew, and restest in the law, and makest thy boast of God**" (2:17). Paul continues his stinging reprimand. The Jews put their trust in having the law and thought that made them right with God. The Jews boasted of having received God's law and were confident they could keep it, but they transgressed the law and could not keep the law they received. God's will was for the Jews to keep His law. Only the perfect Son of God who had the law in His heart could keep God's "more excellent" high standard perfectly. "I delight to do thy will, O my God: yea, <u>thy law is within my heart</u>" (Psa. 40:8). The Jews thought they were teachers of the blind Gentile babes, but <u>they were no better</u>. The Jews were equally guilty and morally corrupt. Do you who teach others know you break the laws you preach? Do you steal or commit adultery? You who abhor idols are you worshipping something besides the true God? <u>The Jews had a form of knowledge in the law, but they did not have the true knowledge of God</u>. For the name of God is blasphemed among the Gentiles through your hypocrisy as written in <u>Isa. 52:5</u>. Which made their physical circumcision worthless. <u>True circumcision is that of the heart and spirit (Deut.10:16)</u>. God is looking for a circumcision of the heart by faith, to believe that what God said about His Son is true. Shall not the uncircumcised Gentiles when they do what the law says judge you as having transgressed the very law you received? Paul said the Jews do the same sins they accuse the Gentiles of. A Jew that is circumcised in heart and in the spirit by faith will have praise of God (2:28, 29). <u>Faith takes place in the heart when a decision is made to believe</u>.

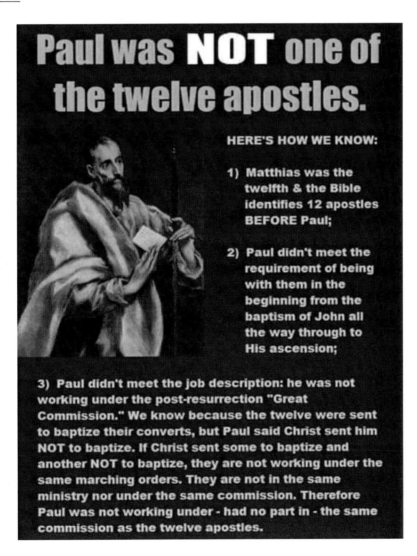

**Romans Chapter 3 The whole world under sin and justification explained**

**3:1-8** What advantage is it then to be a Jew? What is so good about circumcision? The Jews had the advantage in every way. The foremost advantage of all was that unto the Jews (the circumcision) were committed the keeping of the oracles of God (the word of God). <u>God entrusted them with receiving, writing, and making a multiplicity of copies of the Hebrew Old Testament and the New Testament outside of Paul's epistles.</u> The local Gentiles churches are to be "the pillar and ground of the truth" (1 Tim. 3:15) and is also to make a multiplicity of copies of the word of God and translate it. What if some Jews did not believe? Does their unbelief make the faith of God without effect? God forbid, absolutely not! Even if some did not believe, God is still true. Let what God says and does be true and every man a liar that God might be justified when He judges (3:4). God was just to impute His righteousness to David so that David's sins did not condemn him to hell (2 Sam. 12:9, 13). Their unbelief does not affect that God decided to impute His righteousness. God was faithful and His Son paid for all mankind's sins. God will judge righteously. But if our unrighteousness shows that God is righteous, what shall we say? Is God unrighteous to take vengeance on the unbelievers? (Paul said he is asking a foolish question as a man would.) Not at all. How shall God judge the world if there is no right and wrong? If the truth of God is made more obvious by my lie and gives Him more glory, why does He judge me a sinner? Paul anticipates some ridiculous arguments that people may pose and he may have heard. Should we not rather continue to do evil (as some slanderously accuse us of saying) that God may be praised? Those who say so justly deserve damnation.

**3:9-18** Paul asks, <u>Are "we" Jews better than the Gentiles?</u> No, because we have proved in this letter that <u>all are under sin</u> (3:9). God through Paul sums up unsaved mankind's hopeless, sinful condition by quoting a series of verses (Psa. 14:1-3; Eccl. 7:29; Psa. 5:9, 10:7, 36:1, 140:3; Isa. 59:7, 8). There is none righteous no not one . . . <u>no fear of God before their eyes of unbelievers.</u> They have together (Jews and Gentiles) become unprofitable. **"There is none that doeth good, no, not one."**

**<u>3:19, 20</u>** Paul writes, **"Now we [Jews] <u>know that what things soever the law saith, it saith to them who are under the law: that every mouth may be stopped, and all the world may become guilty before God. Therefore by the deeds of the law there shall no flesh be justified in his sight: for by the law is the knowledge of sin"</u>** <u>(3:19, 20). Like a mirror the law showed all nations their sin because even Israel to whom God gave it, could not keep it. The law stopped everyone's mouths. The law is a school master to show lost Gentiles their sin and bring them to Christ (Gal. 3:24). The final verdict, is that ALL THE WORLD IS</u>

GUILTY BEFORE GOD. The purpose of the law was for mankind to have knowledge of their sin, not something that man should strive to keep to justify himself before Holy God. God proved that no son of Adam (5:12), Jew or Gentile, could keep the law, both Peter's and Paul's group need His Son's righteousness.

**3:21-31** "But now" after Paul's sudden and miraculous salvation and call to apostleship by the personal appearing of the Son of God to him on the road to Damascus, God has made a dispensational shift and revealed ALL that the Son's blood has accomplished on Calvary through Paul. **But now the righteousness of God without the law is manifested, being witnessed by the law and the prophets;** [God circumvented the law, He removed the law from the equation by going through the sacrificial system! The law (the five books of Moses) and the prophets (the rest of the OT) witnessed that God was righteous to do so. Jesus believed the Father would do what He said and raise Him from the dead (Psa. 16:10).] **Even the righteousness of God which is by faith of Jesus Christ unto all and upon all them that believe: for there is no difference:** [God imputes the righteousness of His Son "unto all and upon all them that believe" in time past and in the present (3:25, 26). There is no difference in justification or salvation. Christ had the faith and obedience to go through with the Father's plan of redemption, the Son knew He was born for the purpose of dying in man's place (Matt. 20:19; Luke 18:31-34; 1 Cor. 11:23-25; Phil. 2:8; Heb. 10:5). Because of the faith of Jesus, God was able to impart His righteousness] **For all have sinned, and come short of the glory of God;** [There is no difference in condemnation all have come short of His glorious righteous Ten Commandments.] **Being justified freely by his grace through the redemption that is in Christ Jesus: Whom God hath set forth to be a propitiation through faith in his blood, to declare his righteousness for the remission of sins that are past, through the forbearance of God;** [Sinners are justified freely by His grace through the redemptive work of His Son. The Father provided the Son as the propitiation (atonement). Propitiation is the act of appeasing wrath and gaining the favor of an offended person, an atoning sacrifice offered to God to fully satisfy His wrath and render Him no longer angry against man. God was offended by Adam's and our disobedience. The Father had faith that His Son would pay for man's sin with His blood. The law could not justify anyone. God redeemed mankind through the sacrificial system which began in the Garden of Eden (Gen. 3:21) long before the law was given to Moses. The law is the ministration of death; Christ is the ministration of life needed. His Spirit, His life, and His righteousness are the same thing. We receive that GIFT the moment we believe. By one cross God saved two groups. Paul explained that those in Abraham's Bosom (Luke 16:22) could receive His Son's imputed righteousness and be taken to heaven after He rose. Their spirits are currently in heaven (2 Cor.

12:4; Heb. 9:15, 23). Knowing that His Son would redeem and justify believers by the cross with His blood, God forbear or kept back His wrath and did not destroy the <u>Old Testament believers</u> (3:25). <u>Father God's wrath against man's sin was fully appeased and satisfied by His Son's substitutionary blood sacrifice payment, the redemption price</u>). The Father held back His wrath. Christ's righteousness is credited to those who died before the cross in time past in the previous dispensation.] **To declare, I say,** [Paul is the due time testifier (1 Tim. 2:4-6)] **at this time his righteousness:** [At the present time, the Father can remain righteous and declare a believer in Jesus righteous (3:26). Believers in this dispensation receive His imputed righteousness and can be declared righteous by the righteous God.] **that he might be just, and the justifier of him which believeth in Jesus.** [God can remain just, and justly justify the believer in Jesus.] **Where is boasting then? It is excluded. By what law? of works? Nay: but by the law of faith.** [There is no one that can boast because we are saved by faith in Christ and not by keeping the law (which no human could keep). Boasting is excluded because Christ kept the law perfectly and did all the saving. It is excluded by the "law of faith" (8:2), we only believed what He did.] **Therefore we conclude that <u>a man is justified by faith without the deeds of the law</u>.** [A man is justified by faith alone without deeds (works). No one could be saved by keeping the law because everyone had the sinful flesh.] **Is he the God of the Jews only? Is he not also of the Gentiles? Yes, of the Gentiles also:** [Paul answers his own question. Yes, He is the God of the Gentiles also. God justifies the circumcision (Israel) by faith, and the uncircumcision (Gentiles) through faith. Faith without works is what justified both Israel and the Gentiles.] **Do we then make void the law through faith? God forbid: yea, we establish the law.** [The law showed the perfect standard of God's righteousness, which only the Son could keep because it was already in His heart (Psa. 40:8b). Christ's redemptive work established the law.]

**Romans Chapter 4 Imputation explained using Abraham**

**4:1-25** Paul spends an entire chapter to illustrate God's solution to man's sin problem, His Son's imputed righteousness. Imputation was something that God had done in the past. The Father was able to justify others in the past because He had complete confidence that His Son would pay the sin debt. His Son did not disappoint Him, with incomprehensible love, self-sacrifice, and courage He paid the ransom. Abraham and David were justified (received God's imputed righteousness by faith alone) and not by something they did. It is the person that simply believes God and does not think that they can earn their salvation by their own works or righteousness by keeping the law, but trusts in Christ's work on the cross and resurrection, who is saved (4:5). Abraham believed that God would give him many descendants and make a nation out of him just as God had said. Because Abraham believed God, he received God's imputed righteousness, he did not work for it (4:3; Gen. 15:6). When Abraham believed his faith was counted for righteousness. Does this blessedness (imputed righteousness) come only on the circumcision (believing Jews) or on the uncircumcision (Gentiles) also? Since Abraham believed while uncircumcised he is "**the father of all them that believe, though they be not circumcised; that righteousness might be imputed to them also**" (4:11). God gave Abraham the token that proved or sealed the he had while uncircumcised. Therefore, Abraham is the father of all them that believe that righteousness might be imputed to them also. He is the father of those who have faith as he did. Abraham believed and became the "heir of the world" not through the law, but by the "righteousness of faith" (4:13). The law points out sins. Righteousness does not come from keeping the law. "**For if they which are of the law be heirs, faith is made void, and the promise made of none effect**" (4:14). If law-keepers receive righteousness then it is not received by faith, and the promise of righteousness by faith is made of none effect. If we think we must add any of our own works to what Christ has done, we make our faith null and void. If we say we added to our salvation by being water baptized, walking the aisle, confessing our sins, eating a wafer, doing good deeds, and so on, we insult the Father and imply that what His Son did was not enough. Anyone who adds their own work to Christ's finished work on Calvary, is <u>not</u> saved. Therefore, it (imputed righteousness) is of faith by grace. God is gracious to impute His Son's righteousness to the believer and give them eternal life. The promise was to all believers, not just those in the previous dispensation, "**all thy seed**" (4:16). "**(As it is written, I have made thee a father of many nations,) before him whom he believed, even God, who quickeneth the dead, and calleth those things which be not as though they were**" (4:17). People are spiritually dead before they believe and receive Christ's life. God called Abraham the "father of many nations"

(Gen. 17:5) because He calls those things that have not happened yet, as though they had (4:17). God imputed His righteousness to Abraham knowing he would later receive His Son's perfect righteousness. David's sins could only be forgiven if he had God's imputed righteousness. God did not impute iniquity to David because God had already imputed righteousness, His Spirit (sure mercies) to David, (4:6-8; 2 Sam. 12:9, 13; Psa. 32:1, 2). God demonstrated the extent of His forgiveness with King David, he is blessed and will have eternal life in the kingdom. Abraham did not look at his or barren Sara's old functionally dead bodies, but believed what God said. Abraham was "strong in faith" and "fully persuaded" (4:20) that God was able to give him the promised descendants. Faith is to be fully persuaded that what God said is true. Therefore, because of Abrahams's faith, God "**imputed to him for righteousness. Now it was not written for his sake alone, that it** [righteousness] **was imputed to him; But for us** [the body of Christ] **also, to whom it shall be imputed, if we believe on him that raised up Jesus our Lord from the dead; Who was delivered for our offences, and was raised again for our justification**" (4:22-25). We are saved and justified when we believe that Jesus our Lord was delivered for our offences and was raised for our justification. Imputation was in God's word all along (Gen. 15:6; Psalms 32:1, 2), but until Paul was saved, God did not bring to the forefront His solution to man's sin problem. Even now Satan tries to hide it (2 Cor. 4:3, 4).

HOW DO WE EARN RIGHTEOUSNESS?

WE DON'T.

"But to him that worketh not, but BELIEVETH on him that justifieth the ungodly, his FAITH is counted for righteousness."
ROMANS 4:5 KJV

**Romans Chapter 5 Result of justification**

**5:1-11** "**Therefore being justified by faith, we have peace with God through our Lord Jesus Christ: By whom also we have access by faith into this grace wherein we stand, and rejoice in hope of the glory of God**" (5:1, 2). The result of justification by faith is "peace with God through our Lord Jesus Christ." We rejoice knowing that our sins are totally taken care of at Calvary. Since we have Christ's imputed righteousness we can come and stand before the Holy Father without being obliterated. We have access to the Father and our standing by grace is perfect because of Christ's imputed righteousness by faith. We rejoice in hope of the glory of God in heaven (2 Cor. 5:1). We can relax because we have been set free from having to be punished for our sins. We glory in this present life which is preparing us for heaven. Our trials help us to grow spiritually. We glory in our infirmities (2 Cor. 12:9) or difficulties, because tribulations make us patient as we experience the doctrine working in us (2 Cor. 4:17, 12:9; 6:17). We are not ashamed of our hope because "**the love of God is shed abroad in our hearts by the Holy Ghost which is given unto us**" (5:5). Having the Holy Ghost, we have His love for God. Paul began the letter by saluting us from the Father and Son who are in heaven and the Holy Ghost is in us. (Paul has mentioned all three Persons of the Godhead.) We had no power to save ourselves. Some would perhaps dare to die for a good man. But God loved us and Christ died for us while we were yet sinners. "**But God commendeth his love toward us, in that, while we were yet sinners, Christ died for us**" (5:8). Being now justified by His blood and having received His righteousness, believers will not incur God's wrath (hell and the Tribulation) against unbelievers (1:18; 2 Thess. 1:9; 1 Thess. 1:10, 5:9). The Father was reconciled to us by the death of His Son when we were His enemies (lost), but now that we have accepted God's friendship by believing we have His life working in us in this present life (5:10). We have joy because we have been reconciled to the Father and have atonement (friendship takes two) now (in this dispensation) and His eternal life from the moment we were saved (5:11). If we have the imputed righteousness of Jesus Christ, what else do we need? The answer is nothing.

**5:12-21 Our justification "in Christ" is compared and contrasted with the condemnation we had being "in Adam."** Having talked about our sins (the wrong things we do), in this last section Paul speaks of sin (our sin nature). Sin entered the world through one man Adam and passed to all men (5:12). (However, the fact that God did not destroy Adam and Eve immediately meant that God had a plan.) The "similitude of Adam's transgression," Adam transgressed a clear rule or commandment of God. Men died in their sins even before the law was given to Moses. Adam is a "figure" of Christ. Adam is the federal head of lost mankind, while Christ is the federal head of saved mankind. Being "in Adam" is compared and contrasted with being "in Christ" to justification. **"For if by one man's offence death reigned by one; much more they which receive abundance of grace and of the gift of righteousness shall reign in life by one, Jesus Christ."** (5:17). The free gift believers receive is the "gift of righteousness." We can reign in this life and the life to come because of the gift of the Son's righteousness. Adam's sin condemned, Christ's free gift is available to all men unto justification of life. **"For as by one man's** [Adam's] **disobedience many were made sinners, so by the obedience of one** [Christ's] **many were made righteous"** (5:19). Moreover, the law entered that sin may abound, but where sin abounded, grace did much more abound. One man brought sin, another righteousness. Sin reigned unto death, but grace reigned through His righteousness unto eternal life by Jesus Christ our Lord. Salvation is not just-as-if-I-never-sinned, no having the gift of His Son's imputed righteousness is much greater, it is abounding eternal perfection.

**"In Adam" or "in Christ"?**

| Adam and the Law Comparison | Christ and Grace |
|---|---|
| By one man's offence death passed upon all men | Christ's free gift, His righteousness, (5:17) by grace abounded unto many |
| By one man's sin came condemnation | Free gift of justification from offences |
| By one man's offence death reigned | Gift of righteousness by grace by One |
| By the offence of one judgment came upon all men to condemnation | By the righteousness of one the free gift came upon all men to justification |
| Moreover the law entered that sin may abound (make sin more obvious) | Because of Christ, where sin abounded, grace did much more abound |
| As sin hath reigned unto death | So might grace reign through righteousness unto eternal life by Jesus Christ our Lord |

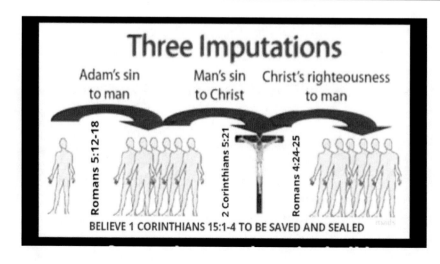

**Romans Chapter 6 Our new identity in Christ**

**If we believe in the right doctrine, then we are now able to live a life of <u>service to God</u>.** Satan knows that if we believe that the body of Christ began in Acts 2 that we will put ourselves back under the law, activate sin in our lives, think water every time God says baptized, and be functionally useless in our service to God. But if we believe that the body of Christ began with Paul's salvation on the road to Damascus in Acts 9 then we will understand His distinct apostleship, be spiritual, and be useful to God now and in the future (1 Cor. 14:37). (See chart on page 59)

**6:1-14** <u>How shall we then live?</u> If Christ's righteousness abounds more than Adam's sin, should we sin more so grace abounds more? God forbid! NO, God did not save us to sin, but to give us Christ's life so we can serve Him. We are dead to sin, set free from sin, and should no longer live in sin. WE ARE DEAD TO SIN (6:1-2), but ALIVE UNTO GOD (6:3-11) through our Lord Jesus Christ, so we can live a life of service to Him. Paul explains our Spiritual identification with Christ upon salvation. **"Know ye not, that so many of us as were baptized into Jesus Christ were baptized into his death? Therefore we are buried with him by baptism into death: that like as Christ was raised up from the dead by the glory of the Father, even so we also should WALK in newness of life"** (6:3, 4). We have been baptized into His death (our <u>old man</u> that we had when we were in Adam was crucified). Buried with Him (our sin put away). Raised with Him in newness of life. <u>The power of sin in our life is broken as we walk in newness of life (not our life, His life) under grace, not the law.</u> We now have the "<u>new man</u>," Christ's Spirit (Eph. 4:23, 24; Col. 3:10). **"Knowing this, that our <u>old man</u> is crucified with him, that the <u>body of sin</u> might be destroyed, that <u>henceforth we should not serve sin</u>"** (6:6). <u>The only remedy for the old man is destruction by crucifixion, he cannot be reformed.</u> He died once. **"Likewise <u>reckon</u> ye also yourselves to be <u>dead indeed unto sin, but alive unto God</u> through Jesus Christ our Lord"** (6:11). We know that Christ was raised from the dead, and He is in us. We are to KNOW, RECKON, and YEILD to what God said. We know we are dead to sin and have been identified with His death, burial, and resurrection (DBR). <u>We reckon or count on what God said about us is true</u>. It was a spiritual operation so we did not feel it (Col. 2:12). We yield our members, our bodies to God (12:1, 2), for His life to live through us in service to Him as His heaven-bound people. Therefore, decide to no longer allow sin in your life (just <u>say no</u> to sin). Yield yourselves as servants to God, as those who are alive from the dead. We were useless to God before we were saved, now we use our body as <u>instruments of righteousness</u>. Do not let sin rule you because <u>you are not under the law that activates sin, but under grace</u> (6:14). By His grace we have His Son's life operating in us, so serve God out of love as sons. As children, we obeyed our mortal fathers out of fear of punishment but when we became adults we obeyed them out of love knowing what was right and did not need the rules. (We should not want to go back to being under the rules.) We walk by faith in His words to us (Romans to Philemon) and the rest of the Bible knowing it was not to us but for our learning.

**6:15-23** "**What then? shall we sin, because we are not under the law, but under grace? God forbid**" (6:15). Shall we sin because we are under grace? God forbid because if we serve sin then sin will be our master and we will die functionally to God, but His Spirit in us is obedient unto righteousness. You used to serve sin, but then you obeyed (believed from the heart) the form of doctrine Christ through Paul gave for His heavenly people. You are free from sin and servants unto righteousness. <u>Living by faith in Christ's doctrine that Paul delivered to us is the SOLUTION</u> (6:17). "**Being then made free from sin, <u>ye became the servants of righteousness</u>**" (6:18). Paul makes his point clear as he asks the questions men would pose and he may have heard. Decide to serve righteousness, yield to His Spirit in you, not your flesh. When you served sin you were free from righteousness and your fruit was shameful and dead. But now, being free from sin use your body to serve God in righteousness having "**fruit unto holiness, and the end everlasting life**" (6:22). Serving sin results in functional death "**but the gift of God is <u>eternal life through Jesus Christ our Lord</u>**" (6:23). We cannot produce any <u>fruit</u> of righteousness that pleases God without the life of Christ working in us and understanding the (indoctrination) form of doctrine Christ gave us through Paul (Gal. 5:22, 23). Do God's will and serve Him and reap eternal rewards (1 Tim. 2:4, 4:8), because the wages of sin (activated by the law) is functional death.

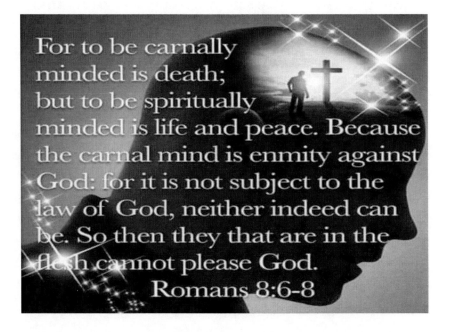

## Romans Chapter 7 Our new problem in the flesh

We are dead to the law (a dead man cannot be brought to trial), but we still have the no-good sinful flesh in our bodies. This is very useful information to know because otherwise, we would wonder why we still sometimes sin after we are saved. (I recommend reading this chapter in our Romans commentary.) The law can condemn a man and activate his sinful flesh and render him not functional for service to God. (Paul speaks of this struggle in Galatians 5:16-26.)

**7:1-6** Paul uses himself as an example of what happens to a believer if they try to live by placing themselves back under the law. The law had dominion over us when we were in Adam. We are DEAD TO THE LAW (by identification with His DBR) and no longer married to it. Christ set us free so we can be joined to Him. Serve righteousness in the newness of the Spirit; not by trying to keep the law.

**7:7-25** The law revives the dead sin nature. Paul uses himself as an example to help believers avoid the pitfall of the Galatians. Paul said that he was functionally alive under grace at one time, but when he put himself back under the law he became functionally useless or dead to God. There was nothing wrong with the law, it was holy, just, and good (7:12). The problem was that the law made the dead sinful flesh that resided in Paul (and us) revive and become "exceeding sinful" (7:13). He did not do the good things he wanted to do; and the evil things he did not want to do, he did. Paul delights in the law of God (His doctrine). But he sees another law in his mortal flesh (carnal) body, the law of sin. The sinful flesh in him wars against the Spirit in his mind to take him captive. Who can free him from this functional death? Exasperated he cried out in self-frustration, "**O wretched man that I am! who shall deliver me from the body of this death** [sin that dewelleth in me, 7:17]**?**" (7:24) Then he answers his own question and continues to answer it in chapter 8. "**I thank God through Jesus Christ our Lord. So then with the mind I myself serve the law of God; but with the flesh the law of sin**" (7:25). Thankfully, we are joined to Christ and receive His Spirit upon salvation, "he that is joined unto the Lord is one spirit" (1 Cor. 6:17). His doctrine in our minds (Eph. 4:23) and hearts help us live right. The law activates the sinful flesh and makes us functionally useless to God. To walk in our old man is contrary to who God has made us in Christ. We cannot serve God in our flesh.

33

**Romans Chapter 8 Our new power in the Spirit**

Because of Christ's Spirit and life in us we can live on a higher plane above sin and self. We are now operating under a new law "the law of the Spirit of life in Christ Jesus" which has made us free from "the law of sin and death" (8:1, 2). We have the ministration of life in Christ and are no longer under the ministration of condemnation and death of the law. He reaches his crescendo, climax in chapter 8.

**8:1-17** "**There is therefore now no condemnation to them which are in Christ Jesus, who walk not after the flesh, but after the Spirit. For the law of the Spirit of life in Christ Jesus hath made me free from the law of sin and death**" (8:1, 2). The law condemned us, it is a ministration of death that activates our sinful flesh. But there is another law for the believer. The "Spirit of life in Christ Jesus" is a ministration of life. We walk in the "Spirit" when we follow the doctrine Christ delivered to us through Paul (6:17). We are dead to sin (6:2). When we walk after the Spirit the law cannot condemn us for we have victory over the flesh. The power of the flesh over the soul has been severed, cut, separated, but the sinful flesh still resides in our mortal bodies and can be activated or revived by the law (7:11). (Man often does what he is told not to do. When the sign says wet paint do not touch, we touch.) The law said you fail to measure up to God's high standard. His life (Spirit) in me bypasses the law. Because we could not keep the law, God sent His Son who did keep it perfectly. Christ condemned sin in His flesh, put sin to death (8:3). When we walk not after the flesh but the Spirit, then we have the righteousness that the law was meant to produce (8:4). His Spirit, His life in us, His righteousness has made us free from sin and death. His Spirit works in us as we let His word rightly divided dwell in us richly (Col. 3:16). We have received His Spirit so we can understand the truth of His word that Christ gave to Paul. To be carnally minded (like the unsaved) is to be functionally dead. I found that when I mixed Peter and Paul and thought they preached the same thing to the same audience and that the body of Christ began in Acts 2 instead of Acts 9 that I did not have the fruit of the Spirit in my Christian life (Gal. 5:22, 23). But after I divided mystery from prophecy, Christ's message to His heavenly people from His message to His earthly people, then the Spirit of Christ in me produced fruit for His glory. We are useless to God when we walk after the flesh, but we are useful to God when we are in the Spirit. Without the Spirit of Jesus Christ in us we are unsaved (8:9). We are useful when we are in the Spirit (walk by faith in the doctrine given to Paul for us). The Spirit takes over so the power of the sinful flesh is broken, and we are functionally alive unto God. "**And if Christ be in you, the body** [the body of the sins of the flesh (Col. 2:11)] **is dead because of sin, but the Spirit is life because of righteousness. But if the Spirit of him** that raised up

**Jesus from the dead dwell in you, he that raised up Christ from the dead shall also <u>quicken your mortal bodies by his Spirit that dwelleth in you</u>**" (8:10, 11). If Christ is in us, who we were in Adam is dead, but His righteousness, His Spirit is life. <u>Christ's Spirit in our present mortal bodies energizes us to be functionally useful to God now (Phil. 2:13), not just in heaven in the "ages to come"</u> (Eph. 2:7). You do not owe the flesh anything, because if you live after it you will die and be functionally useless to God (8:12). **"For if ye live <u>after the flesh</u>, ye shall die: but if ye <u>through the Spirit do mortify</u>** [put to death] **<u>the deeds of the body</u>** [sinful flesh]**, <u>ye shall live</u>**" (8:13). The deeds of the flesh are mortified when we are in the Spirit. Let His Spirit in you put to death the sinful deeds of the body and live unto God. (Turn off the TV and study the Bible RD, so you can serve God and have a better eternal position in heaven.) We must choose to walk after the Spirit, and not <u>after the flesh</u>. We live by faith in the words that Christ gave to Paul. **"For as many as are led by the Spirit of God, they are <u>sons of God</u>**" (8:14). We are sons of God and able to work in the family business when we are in the Spirit. <u>As a child, we obey our parents out of fear of punishment, but as adult sons, we obey out of love and respect.</u> **"For ye have not received the <u>spirit of bondage again to fear</u>; but ye have received the Spirit of adoption** [the Spirit of the Son of God's love for His Father]**, whereby we cry, <u>Abba, Father</u>**" (8:15). <u>The "spirit of bondage" is the spirit of fear of punishment that the law produces.</u> The law was bondage and before we were saved we could not keep it, but after we are saved we naturally keep it (1 Tim. 1:9). <u>It is when we live in the Spirit that we have the mind of Christ (1 Cor. 2:16). We have already received the Spirit of adoption</u> (we have the Spirit of adoption, but our actual son placement or adoption will take place after the Rapture. At the Judgment Seat of Christ, we will be evaluated for job placement in the family business). With His Son's Spirit in us, we can intimately cry <u>Abba, Father</u>, and call the Holy Father our Daddy. The Father loves us too. We have a personal loving relationship with the Father. The Spirit itself testifies witnessing to our spirit that we are His children and if children then we are heirs of God and joint-heirs with Christ. **"The Spirit itself beareth witness with our spirit, that we are the children of God: And if children, then heirs; heirs of God, and joint-heirs with Christ; <u>if so be that we suffer with him, that we may be also glorified together</u>**" (8:16, 17). How do we suffer with Him? We suffer because we live in a fallen body in a fallen sin-cursed world (Eccl. 9:11; Gal. 1:4), but mainly for proclaiming Paul's doctrine. We suffer because we want people to be saved and to come to the knowledge of the truth as we have (2 Tim. 3:12). We suffer with Him because the world hates Him and will not have anything to do with Him, His message, or His followers. We suffer because He just wants the best for His creatures and loves them, but they reject Him, and His word rightly divided. We will receive glory along with His glorious, exalted Son as His joint-heirs.

**8:18-25** "**For I reckon that the sufferings of this present time are not worthy to be compared with the glory which shall be revealed in us.**" The things we suffer for Pauline doctrine in this present time, the dispensation of grace, are not worthy to be compared with the glory which shall be revealed in us (what His Sprit in us did). "**For the earnest expectation of the creature <u>waiteth for the manifestation of the sons of God</u>**" (8:19). All living things are waiting to find out who the sons of God are. Once the sons of God in mystery and prophecy (John 1:12) even angels (Job 38:7) have been revealed then the creatures (animals) that were subject to the sin-cursed corruption of the ground (Gen. 3:17) because of Adam's sin, will be liberated and restored along with all creation. "**For we know that the whole creation groaneth and travaileth in pain together until now.**" (8:22) All creation is <u>groaning</u> with labor pains to be restored and restituted to God's perfect creation, a new heaven and a new earth. "**And not only they,** [the creatures] **but ourselves also, which have the firstfruits of the Spirit, even we ourselves <u>groan</u> within ourselves, waiting for the adoption, to wit, the redemption of our body** [Rapture]" (8:23). We groan trying to get His message of the mystery out to a fallen world, in a fallen body. We, sons of God in mystery who have received the first deposit of the Spirit are waiting for our adoption (placement into our heavenly jobs). <u>We are saved from despair because of the hope</u> (earnest expectation) that God will redeem our bodies at the Rapture and our heavenly rewards for His glory as we live to serve Him. We do not see our places in heaven but wait patiently.

**8:26, 27** "**Likewise the Spirit also helpeth our infirmities: for we know not what we should pray for as we ought: but the Spirit itself maketh intercession for us with groanings which cannot be uttered.**" The Spirit also helps us in our infirmities (weaknesses), for we do not know yet what to pray for so we can serve Him as mature, useful sons of God. <u>The Spirit intercedes and searches our hearts knowing God's will, He helps us serve God according to His purpose</u>. Paul had not received the entire revelation of the mystery yet, but as he received more revelation he knew how to pray (Eph. 1:15-23, 3:14-21; Phil. 1:9-11, 4:4-9; Col. 1:9-20). We have a complete Bible. God will gather heaven and earth into one (Eph. 1:9, 10).

**8:28-30** "**And we know that all things work together for good** [the will of God] **to them that love God, to them who are the called according to <u>his purpose</u>. For whom he did foreknow, <u>he also did predestinate to be conformed to the image of his Son</u>, that <u>he might be the firstborn among many brethren</u>. Moreover whom he did predestinate, them he also called: and whom he called, them he also justified: and whom he justified, them he also glorified**" (8:28-30). God uses the <u>sufferings</u> of this present time to mature us and prepare us to serve Him now and in heaven (2 Cor. 4:17, 18; 1 Tim. 4:8). <u>God foreknew and</u>

purposed that He would have a group called the body of Christ to serve in heaven with Him. He has "chosen us in him before the foundation of the world" (Eph. 1:4). God decided to give them His Son's Spirit. The Godhead had predetermined that His heavenly group was to be conformed to the "image of His Son." The doctrine (His mind) conforms us to His glory. God did predestinate us (the body of Christ) to be conformed to His Son and to live in heaven. He called us by the gospel, justified us, and will also glorify us (2 Thess. 2:14). We have the glory of His Son's life in us now, ready to be revealed in our new bodies at the Rapture.

**8:31-39 "What shall we then say to these things? If God be for us, who can be against us?"** Answer: No one can take His imputed righteousness from us. **"He that spared not his own Son, but delivered him up for us all, how shall he not with him also freely give us all things?"** (8:32). God spared Abraham's son Isaac but He already gave us His Son and delivered Him to die for us all, so will He not surely freely give us all things? **"Who shall lay any thing to the charge of God's elect? It is God that justifieth"** (8:33). The saved Gentiles (the body of Christ) are God's elect and the Father decided to declare us righteous. Who can then justly bring a legal accusation against God's elect? God chose to save the body of Christ, but He did not determine who would be saved. We have free will to decide to believe or not. **"Who is he that condemneth? It is Christ that died, yea rather, that is risen again, who is even at the right hand of God, who also maketh intercession for us"** (8:34). No one can condemn the believer. The answer to man's sin problem is sitting on the right hand of the Father. His very presence there makes intercession for us. His scars are evidence that His redemptive work is done. **"Who shall separate us from the love of Christ? shall tribulation, or distress, or persecution, or famine, or nakedness, or peril, or sword? For thy sake we are killed all the day long; we are accounted as sheep for the slaughter"** (8:36). No one can separate us from the Son who gave Himself for us and rose. We are "killed all the day long" for the cause of Christ. The world does not want Him, His message, or us. But we keep trying to save them and help them to come to the knowledge of the truth so they can understand what God's word says. Satan views us as "sheep for the slaughter" (Psa. 44:22). But we are more than conquerors that put their feet on their enemy's necks **"we are more than conquerors through him that loved us"** (8:37). Paul is persuaded that nothing can separate us from the love of Christ. **"For I am persuaded, that neither death, nor life, nor angels, nor principalities, nor powers, nor things present, nor things to come, Nor height, nor depth, nor any other creature, shall be able to separate us from the love of God, which is in Christ Jesus our Lord"** (8:36-39). Not even another creature (Satan or evil angels) or ourselves can un-save us. God loves His Son more than anything and we are in Him. Once saved, always saved.

**Chapter 9 to 11 Summary - Paul explains God's righteousness and sovereign wisdom in His election of the Gentiles (8:33) and the little flock to fulfill His purpose. Paul tells the believers what has happened to Israel.** (Israel has fallen for a season because they went about to establish their own righteousness. Salvation has temporarily gone to the Gentiles). Through Paul, Christ explains His DISPENSATIONAL CHANGE and that ISRAEL'S PROGRAM HAS BEEN SUSPENDED. Chapter 9: Christ came to Israel but was rejected (9:1-5), but a believing remnant of Israel was saved, Peter's group, the little flock (Luke 12:32). Was God unrighteous to set Israel aside? (9:14) No, God can show mercy to whom He will. If God decides whom He hardens, then how can He fault anyone? Shall a Jewish man question His Maker's decision? He will make a vessel of honor of the believing remnant of Israel. He declared apostate Israel to be in dishonor after being patient with them. Apostate Israel stumbled by not recognizing Jesus Christ. God chose to show mercy to the believing Gentiles and the believing remnant of Israel (9:24, 27). Chapter 10: ISRAEL'S SPIRITUAL STUMBLING and PRESENT SALVATION OPPORTUNITY explained. Paul's heart's desire is for Israel to be saved. Israel's problem was that they thought they could keep the law. They had no idea of God's perfect high unattainable standard which only the Son of God could keep. **"For they being ignorant of God's righteousness, and going about to establish their own righteousness, have not submitted themselves unto the righteousness of God"** (10:3). Paul went throughout the Roman Empire to inform the dispersed of Israel about God's dispensational shift. He let them know that they can be saved into the body of Christ by believing Paul's gospel to the Gentiles. (But in this dispensation the Jews are not above the Gentiles.) God will save anyone that believes that God raised His Son after His satisfactory payment (3:22-26). "Faith cometh by hearing, and hearing by the word of God" (10:17). Peter's group preached the truth to them. But now God was found by the Gentiles who did not seek to be righteous but just believed in Him. While Israel remained disobedient (10:14-21). Chapter 11: ISRAEL'S PRESENT STATE and FUTURE HOPE – DELAYED. Israel's present fall, temporary casting away, and partial blindness (11:1-25). They can be saved by faith as Paul was. God saved a remnant of Jews (Peter's group). Since the little flock is not accepting any new converts they are diminishing. Paul said, **"through their fall salvation is come unto the Gentiles, for to provoke them to jealousy"** (11:11). The fall of Israel was prophesied (Luke 2:34), but not the mystery, salvation going to the Gentiles apart from Israel. **"Now if the fall of them be the riches of the world, and the diminishing of them the riches of the Gentiles; how much more their fulness?"** All believing Israel will be saved at Christ's Second Coming (11:26-29). In His grace, God's present purpose is to save a group to live in heaven. **"God hath concluded them all in unbelief, that he might have mercy upon all"** (11:32).

**Romans Chapter 9 What happened to Israel?**

**Israel fell. God is presently showing mercy to the Gentiles and giving them an opportunity to be saved, God had saved a remnant of Israel (Peter's group).**

**ELECTION**
**Paul primarily writes about <u>nations</u> in these chapters 9-11, <u>not individuals</u>. Election has to do with fulfilling God's purpose, <u>not individual salvation</u>. <u>Election is for service, not salvation</u>. God elects certain nations for His purpose. God's purpose was to bring in His Son, the Redeemer, into the world and save two groups of people. God's purpose stands not because someone worked for it but because God decided to call them. God even <u>used Pharaoh for His service, He uses Satan, and He will use Antichrist</u> for His purpose. Paul explains how God turned from His "<u>chosen people</u>," the nation Israel, to save the Gentiles. Gentiles are all nations. God makes decisions of election depending on His purpose. "Esau is Edom" (Gen. 36:8). "Jacob" is the LORD's (Jer. 51:19). God is using "even us" (9:24) for His purpose.**

**9:1-5** <u>Paul explains that God was righteous to elect to show mercy to the Gentiles</u>. After mentioning that the believing Gentiles are the elect of God (8:33) and the security saved Gentiles have because of the love of Christ (8:35-39), Paul laments over the <u>fall</u> of the nation of Israel. "**I say the truth in Christ, I lie not, my conscience also bearing me witness in the Holy Ghost, <u>That I have great heaviness and continual sorrow in my heart</u>. For I could wish that myself were <u>accursed</u> from Christ for my brethren, my kinsmen according to the flesh**" (9:1-3). Paul has great heaviness of heart and continual sorrow because God has put Israel aside to save the <u>Gentiles</u> to the point that he could wish he was "accursed" (separated from God. That he would never have been saved in Acts 9), and remained <u>cut off from Christ</u> so that his unsaved Jewish "kinsmen according to the flesh" would still be the favored privileged nation of God. Unbelieving Israel is <u>accursed (separated from Christ). Paul could wish it was the other way around</u>. Paul knows that God interrupted His dealings with Israel and began a new dispensation with him. Grace is now abounding to the chief (leader) of sinners. Paul knows that when God saved him on the road to Damascus that He began a <u>new creature</u> or group of believers to live in heaven. In this group, all are one and neither Jew nor Gentile (Gal. 3:28). What matters today is to be part of the new creature (Gal. 6:15). Paul knows that he was the first sinner saved (placed) into the body of Christ. He is a "pattern" for the sinners who will "<u>hereafter</u> believe on Him to life everlasting" (1 Tim. 1:15, 16). But Paul cannot tell God what to do. <u>God decided to temporarily cut off the nation of Israel (Luke 13:9), but a remnant of</u>

Israel was saved and then put on hold (Gal. 2:7-9). Moses asked something similar, for God to forgive those that worshipped the golden calf. "Yet now, if thou wilt forgive their sin—; and if not, blot me, I pray thee, out of thy book which thou hast written" (Ex. 32:32). God let Moses know it was not for him to choose, God will determine how He judges. "And the LORD said unto Moses, Whosoever hath sinned against me, him will I blot out of my book" (Ex. 32:33). But God has mercy on whom He will show mercy (9:15; Ex. 33:19). Paul lists eight of the advantages that Israelites had the last being that Christ came in the flesh as one of them (Gal. 4:4). The covenants all belong to Israel and most covenants are what God on His part will do for them. "**Who are Israelites; to whom pertaineth the adoption** [as sons of God (John 1:12)], **and the glory** [preferred nation], **and the covenants** [all the covenants belong to Israel (Eph. 2:12)], **and the giving of the law, and the service of God, and the promises; Whose are the fathers** [Abraham, Isaac, Jacob], **and of whom as concerning the flesh Christ came, who is over all, God blessed for ever. Amen.**" (9:4, 5). Paul is explaining God's dispensational shift.

**9:6-13** The word of God had taken effect in the remnant of believers in prophecy throughout history. Just because someone is born an Israelite of the seed of Abraham does not mean they are His people. His people are "the children of promise" (spiritual believers in Israel who received His imputed righteousness). Those who are born Jews physically are not the children of God. His children are those of the remnant of Jews with faith in God. These have faith and are counted as His seed just as Abraham and Sara believed God's promise of Isaac's timely birth.

Paul demonstrates God's foreknowledge in election. By grace, God chose to make His nation from Abraham and promised that Isaac would be born through Sara (9:9). In God's foreknowledge, Isaac was chosen to be the seed of promise, not Ishmael. Not only this but when Rebecca conceived twins by "our" (Paul speaks as a Jew) father Isaac, God chose Jacob while the babies were still in her womb and had done nothing good or evil (9:11). The Lord told Rebecca that two nations were in her womb (Gen. 25:23). In the next verse, Paul shows that what God said to Rebecca came true 1,400 years later. "As it is written, Jacob have I loved, but Esau have I hated" (Mal. 1:2, 3). God knew that Esau (the nation of Edom) would not believe Him but that Jacob (the nation of Israel) finally would (during the Tribulation). God hated the nation of Edom because (1) they did not allow Moses to lead Israel through their land, (2) they also asked Israel's enemies to completely "rase" or wipe them out (Psa. 137:7), and (3) Edom rejoiced when the Babylonians took Israel captive (Lam. 4:22; Joel 3:19; Obadiah). Jeremiah prophesied against Edom (Jer. 49:7-22) and spoke of Jacob (Jer. 51:19). Jacob did not work to receive the Abrahamic covenant and the seed line to Messiah, God picked him, elected him before he was born. God told Rebecca, "the elder shall serve the younger." God often picks the second. God will pour out His fury on the Edomites of Mount Seir at His Second Coming because they killed His people out of hatred and envy when the Babylonians came against Israel (Mal. 1:2, 3; Isa. 63:1-4; Ezek. 25:14, 35:11). The people of Edom will have a chance to trust Messiah in the kingdom. But, the man Esau also received a blessing from Isaac (Heb. 11:20).

**9:14-18** What shall we say then is there unrighteousness with God because He picks one people and not another? God orchestrated the seed line from those of His nation by whom the Messiah would come. Now God chose to show mercy to the Gentiles. Was God unrighteous to set Israel aside? Absolutely not. **"For He saith to Moses, I will have mercy on whom I will have mercy, and I will have compassion on whom I will have compassion"** (9:15). God decides in His wisdom to whom He will show mercy and compassion on and to harden whom He will. Paul said that the scriptures said to Pharaoh, that he was raised up for the purpose that God might show His power and His name be declared in all the earth. Paul uses Moses (Ex. 33:19) and Pharaoh (Ex. 9:16) to show that God can decide to show mercy and compassion on who He wants, and to harden who He wants.

How did God harden Pharaoh's heart? The fact that Pharaoh's magicians could duplicate some of God's miracles at the beginning of His judgments on Egypt hardened Pharaoh's heart. The ten plagues of Egypt showed that God was greater than the gods of Egypt. The worship of the underworld, the sun, the river, and so on, could not save them from frogs, flies, gnats, locusts, boils, disease, hail, fire, darkness, the death of their livestock, or of their firstborn. In the past, God has chosen certain people to serve him such as Noah, Abraham, Moses, Pharaoh, the twelve (yet Judas betrayed Him), and Paul. God will use Antichrist (Isa. 10:5, 6) and Satan (Rev. 20:3) for His purposes. God's purpose in election is to call out two groups of people to live eternally with Him, one in heaven and the other on earth.

Is God unrighteous in election? No, God is not unrighteous because He has mercy on the Gentiles and is forming a new agency out of them, the body of Christ. God will yet accomplish His purpose and promise to Israel. His purpose is to save two groups of people by the sacrifice of His Son, to live in two realms (Eph. 1:9, 10). God is not unjust because He picks one and not the other. God can dispense grace and mercy as He chooses. God is not unjust because if God did not show mercy to some, then no one would be saved. God used Pharaoh to serve Him. God uses Satan to see who loves Him. Nobody deserves God's mercy, and no one can condemn God for His choice of forming Israel from the believing remnant. Nor can anyone condemn God for deciding to show mercy to the Gentiles. God hardened Pharaoh and unbelieving Israel. God showed mercy to the Gentiles and the little flock (they will be His holy flock (Ezek. 36:37, 38; 1 Peter 2:9).

**9:19-24** You will ask me then if God picks who He has mercy on how can He find fault with those He hardens? Who can resist His will? No, but who are you O man (Jew) that replies against God? Shall the thing that God formed ask why have you made me this way? "**Hath not the potter power over the clay, of the same lump** [Israel] **to make one vessel unto honour** [the believing remnant or Peter's group which Paul called the "Israel of God" (Gal. 6:16) to differentiate them from the body of Christ.]**, and another unto dishonor** [unbelieving Israel]**? What if God, willing to shew his wrath, and to make his power known, endured with much longsuffering the vessels of wrath fitted to destruction:** [the vessels of wrath are the unbelieving Gentiles (1:18-32) and the unbelieving Jews (Rom. 2) throughout the ages.] **And that he might make known the riches of his glory on the vessels of mercy, which he had afore prepared unto glory, Even us, whom he hath called, not of the Jews only, but also of the Gentiles?**" (9:21-24). God endured the vessels of wrath for the sake of the vessels of mercy "even us" (the body of Christ), not just the believing remnant of Jews (Peter's group). God planned His earthly kingdom "afore" since Adam and Eve (Gen. 1:26, 27). He will use His kingdom of priests to reclaim the Gentiles in prophecy (Ex. 19:5, 6; 1 Peter 2:9). God chose the body of Christ before the foundation of the world to reclaim heaven for His glory (Eph. 1:4). Not only was the little flock saved with more members to join them in the Tribulation, but the body of Christ is currently being added to.

The "thing formed" is Israel. Israel was "marred in the hand of the potter" (Jer. 18:4-6, Isa. 19:16). God is the potter. The lump is Israel. Israel was an honorable vessel before the fall, but after their fall in Acts 7, they were dishonorable. So God shaped the nation of Israel to be Lo-ammi (not my people, Hosea 1:8-10) but in the future (after the Rapture) the nation of Israel will be a reshaped lump of clay from the believing remnant and they will be called "the sons of the living God" (Hosea 2:23, 2 Peter 2:9, 10). After the Rapture, God will make the nation of Israel a vessel of honour (preferred nation) out of Peter's group (9:6, 7, 25-33) and the believers added to them during the Tribulation. After the Tribulation, God will give the Kingdom to the believing remnant making the lump and the vessel of 100% pure honour under the New Covenant with His Spirit in them (Jer. 31:31-34; Ezek. 36:24-28; Heb. 8:8). The vessels of mercy are the saved Gentiles and a believing remnant of Israel (8:33; 9:23, 24). Peter's group had been saved into the kingdom on earth (Matt. 19:28). But since the Jerusalem Council only Paul's group is accepting new converts into the body of Christ to live in heaven (Acts 15; Gal. 2:7-9) by God's mercy. Without new converts, Peter's group that existed in Paul's day died out in the first century. But more little flock kingdom saints will be added in the Tribulation. (There is no remnant today because individual Jews today who believe become members of the body of Christ).

**9:25-27 "And it shall come to pass, that in the place where it was said unto them, Ye are not my people;** [Lo-ammi (Hosea 1:8-10, 2:23)] **there shall they be called the children of the living God** [Peter's group]" (9:26). God called the remnant, Peter's group, "my people" before, during, and after the Tribulation. "But ye are a chosen generation, a royal priesthood, an holy nation, a peculiar people; that ye should shew forth the praises of him who hath called you out of darkness into his marvellous light: Which in time past were not a people, but are now the people of God: which had not obtained mercy, but now have obtained mercy" (1 Peter 2:9, 10). God has always had a believing remnant, even in Elijah's day.

**9:27-29 "Esaias also crieth concerning Israel, Though the number of the children of Israel be as the sand of the sea, a remnant shall be saved: For he will finish the work, and cut it short in righteousness: because a short work will the Lord make upon the earth"** Paul quotes Isaiah 1:9 who also said a remnant would be saved. God will make a short work on the earth and will finish the work of finding out who else in Israel will believe in Him during the last seven years of Daniel's timeline of 490 years (Dan. 9:24-27), the Tribulation, or Jacob's trouble (Jer. 30:7). God will save more believers into Peter's group at that time and the people who were not called my people (Peter's group) will be called "the children of the living God." (Jesus Christ will be living on the earth.) All people have free will and are saved by faith and receive His Son's righteousness. God's purpose in election is to save two different groups of people by two different gospels to live in two different places, heaven and earth. God the Father's ultimate purpose is to exalt His Son Jesus Christ in two spheres (Eph. 1:9, 10). God's purpose in ELECTION is to spend about 7,000 years to find out who will live for eternity in heaven and on earth. Paul quotes Isa. 10:22 that says that a remnant of Israel will be saved (Isa. 4:2-4; Zech. 13:8, 9). The context is the Tribulation when the Antichrist is trying to convert all of Israel to his false religion. It is important to note this context because there is no "remnant of Israel" right now since Peter's group was put on hold nearly 2,000 years ago. Why will God cut the work short on earth? The Tribulation will only be seven years because "except those days should be shortened, there should no flesh be saved" (Matt. 24:22). No one would survive. Unless the "God of Sabaoth" had left us a seed (believing remnant) Israel would have been wiped out like "Sodoma" and "Gomorrha" (Isa. 1:9-11). God was not pleased with Israel because of their unbelief and their own religious traditions. God was not unfaithful to Israel, but rather Israel was unfaithful to God. At Christ's

Second Coming, Israel will be in the same condition they were in at Christ's first coming. His prophesied wrath gets Israel's attention. The believing remnant will have hope in the Tribulation because they will know from scripture that God Raptured the body of Christ (2 Thess. 1:10). This is why Jesus said that He will "come quickly" (Rev. 22:20), not soon. When Israel's time is up, He will return quickly to bring the believers into the kingdom.

**9:30-33 "What shall we say then? That <u>the Gentiles, which followed not after righteousness</u>, have attained to righteousness, even the righteousness which is of faith. But Israel, which followed after the law of righteousness, <u>hath not attained to the law of righteousness</u>"** (9:30, 31). <u>The Gentiles that believe are His elect</u> (8:33; Col. 3:12; Titus 1:1). The Gentiles who did not try to be righteous by keeping the law have "attained to righteousness" by direct faith in Jesus, but the <u>unbelieving in the nation of Israel</u> who tried to be righteous by keeping the law have <u>not</u> attained to righteousness. **Wherefore? <u>Because they sought it not by faith, but as it were by the works of the law. For they stumbled at that stumblingstone</u>; As it is written, Behold, I lay in Sion a stumblingstone and rock of offence: and <u>whosoever believeth on him shall not be ashamed</u>"** (9:32, 33). Paul quotes Isaiah 28:16 for the second time. Why did Israel not receive righteousness? Because Israel did not seek righteousness by faith but by the works of the law (they thought they could keep the law and be righteous on their own), they stumbled on the Stumblingstone. They did not recognize that Jesus Christ was the Rock, a foundation stone, a tried or tested stone, a sure foundation, he that believeth shall not make haste (to go to hell) or be ashamed (not be ashamed and go to the fiery furnace but be saved). Israel did not believe in the Stumblingstone, the Rock of offense, their own Messiah. <u>It is offensive to mankind that Jesus Christ alone did all the work of salvation</u>. In the future, God will make the believing remnant of Israel into His nation (Matt. 21:42-44; Luke 12:32).

44

**Romans Chapter 10 Present salvation opportunity for individual Jews**

**10:1-3** "Brethren, <u>**my heart's desire and prayer to God for Israel is, that they might be saved. For I bear them record that they have a zeal of God, but not according to knowledge**</u>" (10:1, 2). Paul's heart's desire and prayer is that Israel may be saved from their sins by believing the gospel that he preaches (10:8). Paul said that Israel fell because they <u>went about to establish their own righteousness,</u> but now the Jews can be saved into the body of Christ. Israel is zealous (as Paul was before he was saved) but not <u>according to knowledge of His word.</u> Israel thought she could keep the high standard of the law on her own and earn their way to God. They had no idea of God's perfect high <u>unattainable</u> righteous standard which only the Son of God could keep. "<u>**For they being ignorant of God's righteousness, and going about to establish their own righteousness, have not submitted themselves unto the righteousness of God**</u>" (10:3). <u>Israel</u> went about to establish their own righteousness, not the righteousness of God. In so doing <u>they</u> did not submit themselves "<u>unto the righteousness of God.</u>" God's perfect righteousness is received, not achieved (4:5). It is the same for believers today if they add any of their own work to the finished work of Jesus Christ (such as water baptism, keeping the law, confessing their sins) they make their "faith of none effect" (4:14). Because they insult God by saying that what Christ did was not enough and they will not be saved. We should not go about to establish our own righteousness, we trust what Christ has done. Israel did not believe they needed a Redeemer because they thought they could keep the law.

**10:4** "**For Christ is the end of the <u>law for righteousness</u> to every one that believeth**" (10:4). Paul does not say Christ is the end of the law, but that "<u>Christ is the end of the law for righteousness.</u>" If Israel had believed they would have <u>received Christ's righteousness. The Son kept God's law perfectly</u> (Psa. 40:8). Jesus Christ is the answer to receiving absolute perfect imputed righteousness. A saved person has believed and a lost person has either <u>not heard the gospel or heard it and not believed it</u> (rejected it). It is His righteousness that is needed. Faith in Him is the way to receive His righteousness. In the future dispensation, Israel will call the Lord Jesus Christ "THE LORD OUR RIGHTEOUSNESS" (Jer. 23:6). But Jews in this dispensation can be saved by believing Paul's gospel (3:21-26).

**10:5** Paul quotes Lev. 18:5: "**For Moses describeth the righteousness which is of the law, That the man which doeth those things shall live by them.**" Moses said that if you keep all the law all the time you will be righteous (James 2:10). <u>No human that has inherited the sin nature from Adam can keep the law</u> (5:12). <u>If Israel kept God's law they could be His kingdom of priests, but Israel did not keep</u>

the law, so they could not be His kingdom of priests (Ex. 19:5, 6). They made the golden calf while Moses was receiving the Ten Commandments (Ex. 32:4). But in the future under the New Covenant, they will be able to keep His laws and be His priests. Paul told the Jews in Antioch of Pisidia that they could be justified by faith. "Be it known unto you therefore, men and brethren, that through this man [Jesus, God's Son] is preached unto you the forgiveness of sins: And by him all that believe are justified from all things, from which ye could not be justified by the law of Moses" (Acts 13:38, 39).

**10:6-8** Paul compares the righteousness of the law with the righteousness that is by faith. The righteousness which God requires is found by faith in the gospel "**we preach**." What does the word of God say? Paul said, to have the righteousness which is of faith, do not say in your heart that you need to ascend to heaven to find it (that is to bring Christ down from above), or that you need to descend into the deep [hell (Jonah 2:2, 3)] (that is to bring Christ up from the dead), "**The word is nigh thee, even in thy mouth, and in thy heart: that is, the word of faith, which WE [Paul] PREACH**" (Deut. 30:11-14). Paul said you do not have to go anywhere, Christ is found in God's word, to have His righteousness just believe the gospel "**we preach**." Christ has already come from heaven and risen from the grave just believe what we preach. Israel knew they had to obey Moses, and now they are to obey Paul. There is no need to seek after God some mystical way.

**10:9, 10** "**That if thou shalt confess with thy mouth the Lord Jesus** [He is Christ]**, and shalt believe in thine heart that God hath raised him from the dead, thou shalt be saved** [from the consequences of your sins]**. For with the heart man believeth unto righteousness; and with the mouth confession** [The decision to believe is made in the heart. Believe that Jesus Christ really is the Son of God who died for your sins and that God really did raise Him from the dead] **is made unto salvation.**" (There is no need for an audible public confession salvation is between the individual and God who knows the thoughts of our minds and hearts.) Paul never says we are to confess Jesus Christ before men, we confess or communicate to God that we believe. No public confession is necessary. When Christ speaks about a public confession in Matthew 10:32, He is referring to the remnant of Israel during the Tribulation confessing His name before the followers of Antichrist. In I John 1:9, the nation of Israel is to confess their sin of killing their Messiah and God will forgive them and cleanse the nation at His Second Coming. God sees our heart and wants to see our heart resting in the finished work of Christ. These verses do not expressly say Christ's death for our sins, but "saved" (saved from hellfire, sins consequence). Paul specifically says that "Christ died for our sins" and rose in 1 Corinthians 15:3, 4, therefore those verses should be used in conjunction with these verses when witnessing to the lost. <u>Knowing the facts does not save us, we have to believe the gospel in our hearts.</u>

**10:11-13** Paul quotes Joel and applies it to this present time. "**For the scripture saith, <u>Whosoever</u>** [anyone] **believeth on him shall not be ashamed** [never be disappointed]" (Paul quotes Joel 2:32). **For there is <u>no difference between the Jew and the Greek</u>:** [Gentiles] **for the same <u>Lord</u> over all is rich unto all that <u>call upon him</u>. For whosoever shall call upon the <u>name</u> of the Lord shall be saved.**" There was no difference between those who sinned (3:23), now there is no difference in salvation for those that believe Paul's gospel. <u>Paul says that God is rich to both Jews and Gentiles that call upon Him, imputing the righteousness of His Son to them in this dispensation when they believe what Lord Jesus has done.</u> God is currently extending mercy and will save any sinner that believes the gospel.

**10:14-17** Israel has heard the preaching of Jesus Christ by the believing remnant (Peter's group), but Israel did not all obey (believe) that "gospel of the kingdom." The feet of those who preach the gospel are beautiful because they proclaim the gospel of peace that has the power to save the lost! **How then shall they** [Israel] **call on him in whom they have not believed? "For Esaias saith, Lord, who hath believed our report?"** (10:14, 15; Isa. 53:1). In Isaiah's day, in Christ's earthly ministry, and today, people should hear and believe our report. **"So then faith cometh by hearing, and <u>hearing by the word of God</u>"** (10:17).

**10:18-21** Paul proves that God was righteous to set unbelieving Israel aside. Israel heard Christ preached during Acts first by Peter's group, and then Paul). **"But I say, Have they not heard? Yes verily, their sound went into all the earth, and their words unto the ends of the world. But I say, Did not Israel know? First Moses saith, I will provoke you to jealousy by them that are <u>no people</u>, and by <u>a foolish nation</u> I will anger you.**" Peter's group provoked the nation to jealousy and anger because they thought them foolish to think that Jesus Christ was the Messiah. The <u>no people</u> and <u>a foolish nation</u> will be the nation in the kingdom (Deut. 32:21). **"But Esaias is very bold, and saith, I was found of them that sought me not; <u>I was made manifest unto them that asked not after me</u>"** (10:20, Paul quotes Isa. 65:1). The believing remnant did not ask for Him but found Messiah. **"But to Israel he saith, All day long I have stretched forth my hands unto a disobedient and gainsaying people"** (10:21, Paul quotes Isa. 65:2). But apostate disobedient arguing Israel would not come into His <u>open arms</u>. Israel did not believe Peter's group, <u>but individual Jews can be saved into the body of Christ</u>. (Please see **One Year Extension of Mercy for Israel** in the Appendix)

**Romans Chapter 11 Has God cast away His people?**

**Paul explains Israel's blindness in part during this dispensation.** Has God cast away His people, now that God is showing mercy to the Gentiles?

Who is the wild olive tree that is grafted into the good olive tree? "**For I speak to you Gentiles . . . and thou, being a wild olive tree, wert graffed in among them, and with them partakest of the root and fatness of the olive tree**" (Rom. 11:13, 17). The Gentiles are the wild olive tree because "Gentiles" is the antecedent of the pronoun "thou," the wild olive tree. Notice it is the Gentiles, NOT the body of Christ that are grafted in. God is dispensing grace during Israel's national blindness (2 Cor. 5:19; Eph. 3:2). Jesus is the root (15:12) and the fatness is the oil (Spirit).

**11:1"I say then, Hath God cast away his people? God forbid. For I also am an Israelite, of the seed of Abraham, of the tribe of Benjamin."** (11:1). Now that God is showing mercy to the Gentiles, has God cast away His people? God has not cast away His people because He saved Peter's group and He saved Paul an Israelite, and they can be saved in His new dispensation of grace, just as Paul was saved. Paul committed the unpardonable blasphemy of the Holy Ghost by rejecting the renewed offer of the Holy Ghost filled Messianic kingdom saints (Peter's group) by consenting to the stoning death of Stephen, Israel's last straw (Matt. 12:31, 32; Acts 7:58, 22:20). Paul vehemently persecuted the little flock and tried to stamp them out (Gal. 1:23; Acts 8:1, 9:1, 26:11). Since Paul could not be saved in this world, neither in the world to come (Matt. 12:31, 32, Heb. 2:5), God saved him into a new world or dispensation (1 Cor. 9:27; Eph. 3:2; Col. 1:25).

**11:2-10 "God hath not cast away his people which he foreknew. Wot ye not what the scripture saith of Elias? how he maketh intercession to God against Israel, saying, Lord, they have killed thy prophets, and digged down thine altars; and I am left alone, and they seek my life"** (11:2, 3). God "foreknew" the body of Christ (8:29) and He "foreknew" Peter's group (Gal. 2:7-9). God foreknew He would have a saved nation on earth, and God foreknew that the body of Christ would live in heaven (8:24), but He did not predetermine who would be saved. As in Elias' day when God had a remnant of seven thousand, there is a remnant (Peter's group) according to election of God's grace, not works. They were elected to serve by God's grace and were still alive when Paul wrote this letter (11:5). **"And if by grace, then is it no more of works: otherwise grace is no more grace. But if it be of works, then is it no more grace: otherwise work is no more work"** (11:6). Election for service is by God's grace, not works. **"What then? Israel hath not obtained that which he** [not she] **seeketh for**

[righteousness]; **but the election** [little flock] **hath obtained it, and the rest were blinded (According as it is written, God hath given them the spirit of slumber, eyes that they should not see, and ears that they should not hear;) unto this day. And David saith, Let their table be made a snare, and a trap, and a stumblingblock, and a recompence unto them: Let their eyes be darkened, that they may not see, and bow down their back** [burdened with sin] **alway."** (Paul quotes Psa. 69:23; Isa. 29:9, 10). Peter's group was saved and the rest of Israel were blinded. The prophets foretold the blinding of the apostate nation of Israel. All the privileges God gave His nation Israel became a snare, a trap, and a stumblingblock to him. He is to be paid back for his unbelief.

**11:11, 12** Paul explains Israel's temporary fall and casting away. **"I say then, Have they stumbled that they should fall? God forbid: but rather THROUGH THEIR FALL SALVATION IS COME UNTO THE GENTILES, for to provoke them to jealousy"** (11:11) The "fall and rising again of many in Israel" and His "wrath to come" was prophesied (Luke 2:24, 3:7), but not the mystery. Now God's favor to the Gentiles in mystery causes the Jews to be jealous so that they may be saved in this new dispensation. Israel stumbled at the cross, and then fell in Acts 7, when the religious leaders (who represented the nation) rejected their Messiah by stoning Stephen to death because they wanted to take the nation for themselves by force (Psa. 2:3; Matt. 11:12; Luke 19:14; Acts 7:51-60). The nation committed the unforgivable blasphemy of the Holy Ghost (Matt. 12:31, 32) at the end of their one-year extension of mercy (Luke 13:6-9). Christ also prayed on the cross "Father forgive them" (Luke 23:34). **"Now if the fall of them be the riches of the world, and the diminishing of them the riches of the Gentiles; how much more their fulness?"** (11:12). Through Israel's fall, all the world has a salvation opportunity during the dispensation of grace and access to God without having to go through Israel. The Gentiles can believe directly in what Jesus Christ has done. Can you imagine how many Gentiles will be saved when Israel rises (fulness)? There are two different fulnesses. Israel fell from being God's preferred nation and diminished during Acts. The little flock were placed on hold and agreed NOT to take any new converts at the Jerusalem Council and they died off in the first century (Acts 15; Gal. 2:7-9). Gentiles have received riches (the chance to receive His imputed righteousness and eternal life in heaven). Unbelieving Israel rejected the Holy Ghost filled remnant of believers (Peter's group), and then they rejected the Holy Spirit filled Paul (Acts 13:46, 18:6, 28:28). Paul's frequent visits to the synagogues during Acts were to notify the lost Jews of God's dispensational shift and that they now needed to be saved through his ministry. Israel has fallen temporarily, but God will resume His dealing with them. How much more glorious will their future rise to glory be when the nation is saved at Christ's return? Israel will then evangelize the Gentiles in the millennial kingdom (Matt. 28:19, 20).

**11:13-15** "**For <u>I speak to you Gentiles</u>, inasmuch as <u>I am the apostle of the Gentiles, I magnify mine office</u>: If by any means I may provoke to emulation them which are my flesh, and <u>might save some of them</u>**" (11:13, 14). <u>Paul speaks to the Gentiles and magnifies his office</u> of being the apostle of the Gentiles to provoke the Jews to want to be like the believing Gentiles, so he can save some of them into the body of Christ. "**For if the <u>casting away</u> of them be the reconciling of the world, what shall the receiving of them be, but life from the dead?**" (11:15) The world now has a salvation opportunity. <u>The Father is reconciled to the world through the cross (2 Cor. 5:19), but not all the people have believed and been reconciled to Him.</u> But at Christ's Second Coming to earth to Israel, the kingdom saints will be <u>resurrected from the dead</u>. They and the Tribulation saints will receive <u>glorified bodies with His Spirit in them</u> (Isa. 60:1-3).

**11:16-24** <u>Paul uses the analogy of the olive tree. The doors of the temple were made of the olive tree (1 Kings 6:31-33), there is a "green olive tree" (Jer. 11:16, 17), and two olive trees empty their golden oil by themselves through seven pipes to keep the seven lamps on top of the candlestick burning perpetually (eternally) in Zechariah 4. Therefore, the olive tree seems to represent access to God and the opportunity for eternal life. God has set Israel aside because of their unbelief in the Cornerstone Jesus Christ and their preference for their vain religious system.</u> "**For if the firstfruit be holy,** [the believing remnant, Peter's group] **the lump is also holy: and if the <u>root</u> be holy, so are the branches** [that receive righteousness]. **And if some of the branches be broken off, and <u>thou</u>,** [the Gentiles, NOT the body of Christ] **being a <u>wild olive tree</u>, wert graffed in among them, and with them partakest of the <u>root and fatness of the olive tree</u>;** [the <u>root</u> is Jesus Christ (15:12; Rev. 5:5, 22:16) from whom flows fatness (oil, Holy Ghost, righteousness). The <u>good olive tree</u> is the opportunity to have access to God and eternal life by faith like Abraham (4:5; Gal. 3:14)] **Boast not against the branches. But if thou boast, thou bearest not the root, but the root thee.** [Gentiles should not boast] **Thou wilt say then, The branches were broken off, that I might be graffed in.** [The Gentiles will say Israel was broken off so I could be graft in] **Well; because of unbelief they were broken off, and thou standeth by faith.** [The Gentiles that believe become members of the body of Christ. Israel was broken off because of their unbelief. If you Gentiles believe then you will stand before God.] **Be not highminded, but fear: For if God spared not the natural branches, take heed lest he also spare not thee.** [Do not get highminded but fear, and be warned otherwise God may decide not to spare you] **Behold therefore the <u>goodness</u> and**

**severity** of God: on them which fell, severity; [unbelieving Israel is accursed, separated from God] **but toward thee,** [Gentiles, not the body of Christ] **goodness, if thou continue in his goodness: otherwise thou also shalt be cut off.** [When Gentiles return to globalism the Rapture cuts off this dispensation.] **And they** [Israel] **also, if they abide not still in unbelief, shall be graffed in: <u>for God is able to graff them in again</u>.**" [If Israel does not stay unbelieving then God is able to graft them in again. Observe how severe God was on unbelieving Israel, but good toward the Gentiles if you continue in His goodness, otherwise your salvation opportunity will be cut off. The Rapture cuts off the opportunity to be saved to live in heaven.] **For if thou wert cut out of the olive tree which is wild by nature** [not cultivated]**, and wert graffed contrary to nature into a <u>good olive tree</u>: how much more shall these, which be the natural branches, be graffed into their own olive tree?**" (11:16-24). [Usually, a good branch is grafted in but in this case, an inferior wild branch was grafted into the olive tree. Will not the grafting in of the natural branches into their own olive tree be easier? God will graft in the kingdom saints that believe during the Tribulation and add them to Peter's group.]

**11:25 "For I would not, brethren, that ye should be ignorant of this <u>mystery</u>, lest ye should be wise in <u>your own conceits</u>; that blindness in part is happened to Israel, until the <u>fulness of the Gentiles</u> be come in."** Paul would not have the Gentile believers to be ignorant of the <u>mystery</u> of Israel's blindness in part so they do not get wise in their <u>own conceits. "Your own conceits" is to think you are someone you are not because you are not Israel. Do not be conceited, your chance will not last forever God has a plan for Israel.</u> God blinded them for their unbelief, not because you were great. God has postponed Israel's program and inserted the dispensation of grace. Israel has been blinded temporarily in part (Peter's group was saved) by God until the Rapture. The "fullness of the Gentiles" is when the purpose for which we were saved is full. We will be ready to serve God in our resurrected glorified bodies (Phil. 3:21) with His Spirit and our soul in them. <u>The blinding of Elymas, the false Jewish prophet, "for a season" while a Gentile was saved by apostle Paul is a type of Israel at the present time</u> (Acts 13:6-12).

**11:26-29 "And so all Israel shall be saved: as it is written, <u>There shall come out of Sion the Deliverer, and shall turn away ungodliness from Jacob: For this is <u>my covenant unto them, when I shall take away their sins</u>."** (11:26, 27). Paul quotes Isaiah 59:20, 21. <u>God has not cast away His people permanently, because He has a future plan for them and He will return as He promised</u> (Jer. 33:40-42). All believing Israel will have their <u>national sins</u> taken away at Christ's Second Coming (1 Peter 1:5, 7, 13). At that time, God will put His Spirit and word in believing Israel under the <u>New Covenant</u>. We are <u>NOT spiritual Israel and we</u>

have NOT replaced Israel because God has a future plan for the "Israel of God" (Gal. 6:16). For this reason, Replacement Theology and Covenant Theology are false. "**As concerning the gospel, they are enemies for your sakes: but as touching the election, <u>they are beloved for the fathers' sakes</u>**" (1 Thess. 2:15). Unbelieving Jews object against God turning to the Gentiles through apostle Paul and deny that God considers them to be as uncircumcised Gentiles (Acts 7:51). <u>God had elected Israel to be His "kingdom of priests" (Ex. 19:5, 6) on earth.</u> "Now therefore, <u>if ye will obey my voice indeed, and keep my covenant, then ye shall be a PECULIAR treasure unto me above all people: for all the earth is mine:</u> And ye shall be unto me a <u>kingdom of priests</u>, and <u>an holy nation</u>. These are the words which thou shalt speak unto the children of Israel" (Ex. 19:5, 6). But now, the saved Gentiles are His peculiar people. "Who gave himself for us, that he might redeem us from all iniquity, and purify unto himself a <u>peculiar people</u>, zealous of good works" (Titus 2:14). <u>He will not utterly cast her away</u> (Lev. 26:44). God loves Israel for their fathers' sake, He will not change His mind, He keeps promises (Jer. 31:31-34) to "a chosen generation, a royal priesthood" (1 Peter 2:9).

**11:30-32** "**For God hath concluded them all in unbelief, that he might have mercy upon all**" (11:32). In <u>times past</u>, the Gentiles did not believe God, but <u>now the Gentiles have received mercy</u> (Eph. 2:11-13) because of Israel's unbelief. Even so, <u>Israel does not believe now</u>, but by God's mercy to the Gentiles, Israel may obtain mercy. In His grace, God's present purpose in the dispensation of grace (Eph. 3:1-9) is to give everyone an opportunity for eternal life in heaven. <u>Jews can be saved into the body of Christ</u>. God hath concluded Jews and Gentiles all in unbelief during the dispensation of grace so that He might have mercy upon all.

**11:33-36** "**O the depth of the riches both of the wisdom and knowledge of God! how unsearchable are his judgments, and his ways past finding out! For who hath known the mind of the Lord? or who hath been his counsellor? Or who hath first given to him, and it shall be recompensed unto him again? For of him, and through him, and to him, are all things: to whom be glory for ever. Amen**" (11:33-36). Paul breaks out in a jubilant prayer of thankfulness to God for His brilliant and merciful plan to save as many people as possible. He is amazed that <u>although Israel has fallen the Jews still have a chance to be saved into the body of Christ</u>. No one can plummet the depth of the wisdom and knowledge of our God. His thinking and decisions are past our ability to discover His ways or find out! Who has known the excellent incredible perfect mind of the Lord? Has anyone counseled Him what to do? Who has first given to Him and then been paid back by Him? <u>God is a giver</u>. The Gentiles will have another chance to be saved in the kingdom. Paul praises God and wants all glory to be His forever. Amen.

*The nation of Israel has stumbled, fallen (11:11, 12), is cast away (11:15), blind in part (11:25) and "enemies for your sakes" (11:28) if the Gentiles have replaced Israel as "spiritual Israel" then we are all those things, which does not make sense.

## When I Survey The Wondrous Cross
### By Isaac Watts (1707)

When I survey the wond'rous cross
On which the Prince of glory died,
My richest gain I count but loss,
And pour contempt on all my pride.

Forbid it, Lord, that I should boast,
Save in the death of Christ my God!
All the vain things that charm me most,
I sacrifice them to his blood.

See from His head, His hands, His feet,
Sorrow and love flow mingled down!
Did e'er such love and sorrow meet?
Or thorns compose so rich a crown?

His dying crimson, like a robe,
Spreads o'er his body on the tree;
Then am I dead to all the globe,
And all the globe is dead to me.

Were the whole realm of nature mine,
That were a present far too small;
Love so amazing, so divine,
Demands my soul, my life, my all.

**Romans Chapter 12 How do we live a life of service to God?**

**In chapters 12-16 Paul gives practical instructions for the believers in mystery on how to live unto God. It is good to understand the first three cornerstones of Romans before we present our bodies a living sacrifice for Christ to live through and serve Him for His glory. After we have understood our Justification by faith our standing (Rom. 1-5), our Sanctification our state (6-8), and God's Dispensational change (9-11), then we are ready to serve. God is dispensing grace to the world because of the cross of Christ and will save any sinner who believes what His Son has done before the Rapture. We have been educated in the fundamental doctrine in His word with the help of Christ's life, His Righteousness, His Spirit in us (Chapters 1-11). However, while our standing (1-5) is that we are complete in Christ, but our "state" (Phil. 2:19, 20) (6-8) is our "conduct" or "walk" and needs to match our standing which requires spiritual growth (understanding what God tells us in His word, believing it, and applying it). We have eternal life and His Spirit.**

**Rom. 12:1, 2 "I beseech you therefore, brethren, by the mercies of God, that ye present your bodies a living sacrifice, holy, acceptable unto God, which is your reasonable service And be not conformed to this world: but be ye transformed by the renewing of your mind, that ye may prove what is that good, and acceptable, and perfect, will of God.**" Paul continues the paragraph he began in 11:13 speaking to the Gentiles. He beseeches us based on the mercies of God who has concluded all people in unbelief (11:32), so He can have mercy on all during Israel's national blindness (the dispensation of grace or Gentile salvation opportunity) until the Rapture (Rom. 11:25). We are to present our bodies a living sacrifice for Christ to live through, and to be transformed by the renewing of our minds by His word. We have been set free from sin ruling us as we "walk not after the flesh, but after the Spirit" (8:1, 4), we can live holy lives that prove God's good, and acceptable, and perfect will. God's will in this context, is for Jews and Gentiles to be saved into the body of Christ and live right. We are to know in our mind what God said about us, reckon it to be true in our hearts, and yield our bodies in service to Him. Since Jesus Christ died and rose again for us, it is only reasonable that we should want to serve Him. As the hymn goes "O Jesus, Lord and Savior, I give myself to Thee, For Thou, in Thy atonement, didst give Thyself for me . . . My life I give, henceforth to live, O Christ, for Thee alone," *Living for Jesus* by Thomas O. Chisolm (1917). The "old man" (who we were in Adam) was spiritually crucified with Christ, so now Christ, who is our life, can live His life through us (Rom. 6:3-6; Col. 3:4). Christ who lived a perfect life and kept the law perfectly is the "new man" that now lives in us. We have His Spirit and our own souls. <u>Our bodies are earthen vessels that house a treasure, the life of Jesus in and through us</u> (2 Cor. 4:7-11). The magnitude of what it means to have Christ living through us is hard to understand! But by faith, we believe what the Bible says (Gal. 2:20; Col. 1:27). When we receive our glorified bodies and fly around in heaven the light that shines in us will be His light. <u>This life is not about us, but about Christ and what He has done and serving Him and His people</u>. Christ in us is holy. We are accepted because of Him (Eph. 1:6). Satan is the "god of this world" (2 Cor. 4:4), and the "prince of the power of the air" (Eph. 2:2). We need to make sure that we are not wasting our time and being distracted by worldly pursuits that have no eternal value. We are not to be conformed to this world, we are "<u>to be conformed to the image of his Son</u>" (Rom. 8:29). We conform to Christ by reading, studying, and meditating on His word (Col. 3:16, 17). We are renewing (ongoing) our minds by reading and studying the Bible daily (Eph. 4:22-24; Col. 3:6-13). Then we can have the "mind of Christ" (1 Cor. 2:16) and make the right decisions because we will think like Christ. We need to control our minds moment by moment (2 Cor. 10:5). <u>We need to reprogram our minds with the truth of His word rightly divided</u>. As adults, we need to join into what God is doing, we prove and promote His good, and acceptable, and <u>perfect will</u> (1 Tim. 2:4). We need to walk by faith and be led by the Spirit (2 Cor. 5:7; Gal. 5:16). God's word is now complete, so we do not expect God to speak to us in any other way (Col. 1:25).

**12:3-8 "For I say, through the grace given unto me, to every man that is among you, <u>not to think of himself more highly than he ought to think; but to think soberly, according as God hath dealt to every man the measure of faith.</u>"** Paul gives practical instructions for our service to the believers (12:3-16) because of the "grace given unto me." God made Paul His apostle of the Gentiles. God is good to the Gentiles because of Israel's unbelief not because we are wonderful. The proper way for a believer to think of himself is to not think more highly of ourselves than we ought to think but to think soberly (realistically). God has given everyone the measure of faith which grows as we study His word (10:17). <u>The Romans received the Spirit and sign gifts from the Lord Jesus Christ not because they were special, but for the edifying of the church when it was in its' childhood</u> (1 Cor. 13:8-13). Sign gifts were still in effect when <u>Romans was written in Acts 20 and did not cease until Acts 28</u>. There are many members in our one body or group (1 Cor. 12:12-14). As one body in Christ, we are members one of another, we are on the same team. Each member functions differently in the <u>body of Christ</u> in their service for God. We are one organism, agency, group, or <u>team</u>, the "one new man" (Eph. 2:15). We bring different skills and strengths to the group. Everyone has something to offer or share. Serve others like waiters in a restaurant. <u>We use what we have learned for the benefit of all</u>. Paul mentions several gifts and encourages them to use them well: prophecy, ministry, teaching, exhortation (warning), giving, ruling (governing), and showing mercy.

**12:9-16** <u>Serve the body of Christ</u>. Love is to be genuine without hypocrisy, not false or with an ulterior motive. Hate (detest) evil, as God does, but cleave (cling) to what is good. Be kind with warm affection one to another with brotherly love in honor put others first and not yourself. Be interested in other people and their welfare. The most loving thing we can do is to share the gospel. Do not be lazy in business; be fervent (enthusiastic) serving the Lord. "**Rejoice in hope;** [of the Rapture] **patient in tribulations;** [sufferings] <u>**continuing instant in prayer**</u> [to God often]" (12:12). One type of prayer is to pray the instant a need comes to our minds. Share your resources with others, including money to a worthwhile cause, person, or ministry. Cultivate being hospitable, invite and care for people in your home, or restaurant, etc. Bless <u>them which persecute you: bless, and curse not</u>. Speak well of others, and do not speak badly of them. Be joyful with those who rejoice, and cry along with those who are sad (empathize). "<u>**Be of the same mind one toward another**</u>" (12:16). <u>We in the body of Christ should be thinking the same thing as we follow Paul to follow Christ</u> (1 Cor. 11:1). Treat people kindly regardless of social standing. Be humble and avoid feelings of superiority. Don't think you are something special because we are all sinners saved by God's grace.

**12:17-21** <u>Serve the lost</u>. Do not pay back any man evil for evil. Be honest in your dealings in the sight of all men (have just measurements). Do an honest day's work. As far as it is in your power, live peacefully with all men. Paul gently says, "**Dearly beloved, avenge not yourself**" (12:19), instead, leave room for and trust that God will judge rightly; for it is written, "<u>**Vengeance is mine; I will repay, saith the Lord. Therefore if thine enemy hunger, feed him; if he thirst, give him drink: for in so doing thou shalt heap coals of fire on his head**</u>" (12:19, 20) Paul quotes Deut. 32:35; Prov. 25:21, 22. "<u>**Be not overcome of evil, but overcome evil with good**</u>" (12:21). Show kindness and be nice to your enemies because then they may turn to God, or God will punish them more when He sees their injustice toward you. If we return evil for evil, we have been overcome by evil. But if we do not seek revenge, but do good to all men (Gal. 6:10) including our enemies, then we have overcome evil with good. Then evil has failed to affect our inner peace (Gal. 5:22) and to distract us from God's purposes (2 Cor. 4:5).

*"Rejoicing in hope;*
*patient in tribulation;*
*continuing instant in prayer"*
Romans 12:12 KJB

**Romans Chapter 13 Living with government**

**13:1-4** <u>Obey government</u>. Paul wants every soul to be subject to government laws and orders. Human government was God's idea. <u>God has set up governmental structures (authorities) in heaven and on earth</u> (Col. 1:16; Eph. 1:21). It is the office of government that God has ordained, not the men that fill those offices. Those who resist government and its' structure arranged by God, bring judgment on themselves. "<u>Damnation</u>" in this context is punishment from government for doing wrong, not going to hell. When we politely obey, we are not likely to get in trouble with our government and will be praised for cooperation. Generally, the ruler is there for our good, to protect us. Evil is deterred and restrained by strong rules that are reinforced with punishments. The punishment should fit the crime.

**13:5-11** Paul wants the believers to subject themselves as <u>model citizens</u> to obey the rules and avoid the wrath of authorities, but also in order to have a clear conscience. <u>We should not only obey because the government says so, but because our conscience tells us what is right and wrong</u>. You pay taxes for the cause of maintaining law and order. Therefore, pay your taxes and customs and pay respect to your leaders who do their best to rule righteously. God is the highest authority, therefore there are exceptions, when government disobeys God we should obey God rather than men (Acts 4:19, 5:29). <u>Pay your bills, your monthly payment if you take a loan. Owe no man anything, but to love one another. Love is seeking the other person's highest good. When we love others we fulfill the law. God considers us as adult sons who can do what is right without having to follow a list of rules</u>. More people are won to God by love than arguments. Christians who walk with the love of Christ in them have something that others recognize and want. They are the best citizens and the best witnesses for Christ. <u>He that loves another has fulfilled the law</u> (13:8, 10). Paul lists the last five of the Ten Commandments here because they are the ones that deal with our relationship to others. He mentions all except keeping the Sabbath in his writings. All the Sabbaths are signs for Israel (Ezek. 20:12). <u>When we walk in the Spirit we fulfill the righteousness the law of God was meant to produce</u>. "**Thou shalt love thy neighbor as thyself**" (13:9) briefly sums up these commandments. Love does no harm to others, love is the "fulfilling of the law." God's law was given to show us our sin (3:19, 20; Deut. 31:26). Human nature is self-centered, so the only way we can ever keep God's law is for Christ's Spirit to live through us as we let His doctrine through Paul reprogram our minds.

**13:11-14** "**And that, <u>knowing the time</u> that now it is high time to <u>awake out of sleep</u>**." Knowing the time (the time of Israel's partial blindness when Gentiles have been grafted in, and given an opportunity for salvation based on God's grace). It is this present time of suffering in which we now live (8:18). We suffer because we are surrounded by unsaved people, family, and friends who we want to be saved. God has interrupted and postponed Israel's prophetic program and inserted the dispensation of grace which He began with Paul's salvation in Acts 9 (Acts 9:15; 2 Cor. 5:15-19; 1 Tim. 1:15, 16). Notice the urgency to awake and serve God, time is running out! (1 Cor. 7:29-31). We have a short life on earth (Psa. 90:10, 12; James 4:14) so wake up and share the gospel with unbelievers so they can join the body of Christ and not be left behind at the Rapture and "come to the knowledge of the truth" (1 Tim. 2:4) so they will have some more rewards at the Judgment Seat of Christ (2 Cor. 5:10, 2 Tim. 2:15, 4:8). Before Paul wrote Romans he described our blessed heavenly hope for the body of Christ in other letters so he takes it for granted the Roman believers possess and have read them (1 Cor. 15:51, 52; 2 Cor. 5:1; 1 Thess. 14:16, 17). The last days in the dispensation of grace have been in effect for a long time (2 Tim. 3:1-5). Paul expected Christ's imminent return to Rapture us to come at any time. So now nearly 2,000 years later we are nearer than before. We are looking for our Saviour Jesus Christ to catch us up in the air to Himself, the blessed hope of the Rapture (Titus 2:13). Our time period is not forever, it is short, limited, "**the night is far spent, the day is at hand**" the time when God would have send the Tribulation had not the dispensation of grace begun is far spent. The day or dispensation of grace is here and the day of our Rapture could come at any time. (Israel's day will be at His return to them.) We are living in "this present evil world" (Gal. 1:4), serving our Lord as His ambassadors during a time of apostasy (2 Tim. 1:15) and waiting to be called home to heaven. The day of Christ, when we are with Him, will soon be here. Let us deny ungodliness and use our time wisely. Stop behaving like the lost. "Wherein in time past ye walked according to the course of this world, according to the prince of the power of the air, the spirit that now worketh in the children of disobedience" (Eph. 2:2). **Cast off the works of darkness**" [worldly lusts often done at night]**, and let us put on the armour of light**" (13:12). Live soberly, righteously, and godly as in Titus 2:12. Christ is light. The armour of light is really the "doctrine" (6:17) given to us through Paul and Christ's Spirit living through us (12:2). The amount of sound doctrine a person has in their inner man (spirit and soul) helps us to function effectively. To have the "mind of Christ" (1 Cor. 2:16), we study and believe all the word of God rightly divided so we can know Christ's sound doctrine and use it to fight against Satan's false doctrine. "Put on the whole armour of God [all the word of God rightly divided], that ye may be able to stand against the wiles of the devil" (Eph. 6:11). "**Let us walk** [live] **honestly, as in the day;** [Live as in the day when Christ is with us, not as in the night is when He is not. We are not to waste our time on earth.] **not in rioting** [reveling, partying] **and drunkenness, not in chambering** [immoral lewd indulgence] **and wantonness,** [undisciplined, reckless] **not in strike and envying** [arguing with people, and wanting what they have]. **But put ye on the Lord Jesus Christ, and make not provision for the flesh, to fulfil the lusts thereof**" (13:13, 14). Paul reminds us to keep the flesh in subjection and not let it have a chance to lust (1 Cor. 9:24-27; Gal. 5:16; Rom. 8:1, 4). Decide to walk in the Spirit because the law energizes the sinful flesh (7:13, 8:1, 4). We are to say "No" to our flesh with its' sinful lusts and let Christ's Spirit live in us and through us (7:6, 8:1-4, 13, 12:1, 2). We are in Him and He is in us (Col. 1:27; 2:10). Christ is the light and truth (John 1:9, 8:2, 14:6). The <u>law</u> that we follow now is: "<u>the law of the Spirit of life in Christ Jesus</u>" (8:2). We have the "<u>Spirit of Christ</u>" (8:9) in us. Our salvation was settled when we believed. Now CHRIST IS OUR LIFE as we "<u>walk in love</u>, as Christ also hath loved us, and hath given himself for us an offering and a sacrifice to God for a sweetsmelling savour" (Eph. 5:2). Christ was a pleasant smell to God, and we should be like Him.

**What about Hebrews to Revelation?** These letters are written to help the circumcision in the "world to come [post Rapture], whereof we speak" (Heb. 2:5).

**A Map of Paul's Apostolic Journeys which includes Illyricum**

**Paul was more than a "missionary" because he was the one Apostle chosen by Jesus Christ from heaven to form the body of Christ in this dispensation of grace. His journeys were "Apostolic," he alone says "according to <u>my gospel</u>."**

## Romans Chapter 14 The weaker brother and debatable things

**14:1-4** Having just finished saying the night (the dispensation of grace) is far spent (is towards the end) and "the day" of our "gathering together" (2 Thess. 2:1) unto Him (Rapture) is at hand, Paul explains the weaker brother principle using the issue of food. Accept the weaker brother that does not understand the different way Christ is dealing with the body of Christ and mix Peter and Paul and try to help them (remember we used to be like them). Treat the weaker believer with extra care. If they follow Christ's earthly ministry they will be confused and legalistic. Saints who are NOT strong in Pauline doctrine should be accepted as long as they are willing to learn and be taught. The purpose is to teach them, not to argue about minor issues. Someone who is following Christ's earthly ministry may not want to eat the sausage on their pizza. Pauline believers may eat all foods even that offered to idols, while the weaker brother may abstain and some eat only herbs or vegetables (1 Cor. 8:7-13). Do not despise a person because of what they eat, and let not him who is particular about what they eat judge someone who eats all things. What a person eats or does not eat is not the important thing. If a person has trusted in Christ that is the main thing. God has received us both (1 Cor. 12:12-25). Do not judge other believers regarding debatable things, we do not know their motives. There is liberty in Christ! God will straighten them out with His word. Rather help the believer to follow Christ's ministry from heaven through Paul (16:25) and learn how to be "rightly dividing the word of truth" (2 Tim. 2:15). We are to stand in "the faith" firm in Paul's instruction to us (1 Cor. 15:13).

**14:5, 6** Paul knows that some of the Jewish body of Christ members may find it difficult to stop their customary dietary traditions and feast days and he wants the Gentile believers to be patient with them because God will use scripture to help them sort out these minor issues for themselves over time. Eating or not eating does not commend us to God (1 Cor. 8:8). Paul said, one person believes one day is more important than another, and to others, all days are the same. Now in our day of Gentile opportunity (11:13, 25), we are not under Israel's laws (6:14, 9:4) and all days are alike and important (Col. 2:16, 17). Let everyone be fully persuaded in his own mind in what he believes. We should be fully persuaded in our minds that we are NOT Israel and we have no special holy days (Gal. 4:10, 11; Col. 2:16, 17; Phil. 2:15, 16). The Sabbath was a sign between the LORD and Israel to set them apart from other nations. Whoever did not keep it was to be killed (Ex. 31:12-15). The Sabbath represents the millennium. We cannot force someone to be saved or to come to understand right division. If they have no interest we should look for those who do, but not to give up on them too soon. We do not want to harden them to the gospel or turn them off to the message of grace.

Perhaps they will listen in the future. Even if the time never comes, so be it. They will learn when they get to heaven. Since God does not force saved people to read their Bibles and they answer to God, how much more, then, should we not force weaker brethren to learn the truth of God's word rightly divided. We voluntarily abstain from certain practices for their sake. Some people who are not aware of the dispensation we are living in today, may think that they would be more acceptable to God if they share in Israel's holy days (Gal. 4:9-11). We do all things unto the Lord (Col. 3:23-25).

**14:7-10** None of us lives or dies to himself; we live for the Lord. Whether we live or die we are the Lord's and represent Christ as His ambassadors to others. "**For to this end Christ both died, and rose, and revived, that he might be Lord both of the dead and living** [dead or alive believers]" (14:9). He knows the motives, not us. Why do you judge your brother? Why do you set your brother aside as not important? "**for we shall all stand before the judgment seat of Christ**" (14:10). Christ will judge us all for service at the judgment seat of Christ. We are not to judge each other, or even ourselves (1 Cor. 3:8-15; 4:3-5). God's word is "like a fire" the perfect standard measure by which all things will be judged (Jer. 23:29). God does the work through us, and we get the reward, so we will then give Him all the glory! We are in training here, for reigning there! (2 Cor. 1:14, 5:9, 10; Col. 3:24, 25, 2 Tim. 2:12). Our motivation is love and gratitude for His loving sacrifice of Himself for us. His love compels us to allow Him to do good works through us (Gal. 2:20). We live and die unto the Lord, for we belong to Him. We are His "purchased possession" (Eph. 1:14), bought with His blood (Acts 20:28; 1 Cor. 6:19, 20). That is grace! Grace is unearned and undeserved favor. Our operating system is love because of His grace, not the law (2 Cor. 5:14).

**14:11-17** Everyone will bow their knee to the Son of God and confess that Jesus Christ is the LORD (Phil. 2:10, 11). We will gladly bow at His Judgment Seat. Saved Israel shall bow to Him and glory (Isa. 45:23-25). We will all personally give an ACCOUNT to God for how we spent our time on earth. Let us, therefore, not judge another believer's ministry, but instead, make sure we do not cause them to stumble or prevent them from understanding what God is doing today so they can receive a reward at the Judgment Seat of Christ. We are to be concerned with their spiritual well-being and seek to make the weaker believer stronger. When we use the mind of Christ (1 Cor. 2:16) to judge all things, then we judge righteously. Paul is certain that there is no food that is unclean of itself (the best meat was offered to idols). Paul knows it was just meat, the devils (fallen angels in the second heaven) behind the idols do not affect the food. Under grace, we have the liberty to do all things (Gal. 5:1), but not everything is expedient or profitable (1

Cor. 6:12). But if your brother in Christ is concerned about eating food offered to idols then if you serve him that you are not being charitable (loving). Do not ruin another man's spiritual walk by what you eat or drink (1 Cor. 8:7-13). Christ died for them. "For, brethren, ye have been called unto liberty; only use not liberty for an occasion to the flesh, but by love serve one another" (Gal. 5:13). "**Let not our good be evil spoken of**" (14:16). Let not our good suffer because of our thoughtlessness. Our "good" is sharing the gospel and the wonderful, liberating sound doctrine found in Paul's epistles (Col. 1:20-26). "**For the kingdom of God is not meat and drink; but righteousness, and peace, and joy in the Holy Ghost**" (14:17). Paul wants righteousness, peace, and joy among believers. Focus on the things God is doing, not on petty things such as what a man eats or drinks. What we ourselves eat should be irrelevant. God cares about people receiving His Son's righteousness by faith and having peace and joy in the Holy Ghost (3:22, 5:1). When the lost are saved and come to the knowledge of the truth (1 Tim. 2:4), they "rejoice ever more" (1 Thess. 5:16) over being forgiven of their sin, being seated with Christ in the heavenly places, given all the spiritual blessings, and Christ living in them (Eph. 2:6, 1:3; Gal. 2:20). That is why Paul says, "If meat make my brother to offend, I will eat no flesh while the world standest, lest I make my brother to offend" (1 Cor. 8:13). Let us concentrate on eternal things.

**14:18-23** Serve God spiritually. He that thoughtfully, lovingly, courteously, kindly, lovingly, minister to others with righteousness, peace, and joy are acceptable to God, and approved of men. Keep the peace and edify others by helping them mature in the word of God rightly divided. Paul wants peace between Jews and Gentiles in the body of Christ and between strong and weak believers. Sometimes it is best to go along with things we know really do not matter in order to keep the peace so we can have a chance to edify. For example, we may not want to serve pork chops to brothers or sisters who believe they are to follow Israel's dietary laws. So as to not offend them and to have more of a chance to edify the person on eternal matters later, we may serve them chicken instead. We are adult sons of God and stronger brothers because of the sound doctrine we have learned from Paul. Our conduct is to be on a higher plane, as we walk by faith, and not by sight. Do not destroy the work of God because of food. God is patiently working in the weak believer to make him stronger. It took us a long time to come to the truth and it will them. It is fine to eat all foods, but not everyone knows this and may be offended. We should voluntarily abstain from certain dietary practices for the sake of the weaker brother. If you know we have the liberty to eat all things, keep it to yourselves, but if a weaker brother thinks you are eating something that is against God's law, that could wound his conscience (2:15). It is a sin to go against our conscience.

**Romans Chapter 15 Paul's Ministry to the Gentiles**

**15:1, 2** Other's "infirmities" in this context is the following of religious rules by those <u>weak</u> in Pauline sound doctrine. We should put up with the weaker brother that may hold onto Jewish traditions and not think only about ourselves, so we may have a chance to do good and edify them. We all used to be mixers of Peter and Paul or weaker brothers, but now we are stronger brothers and sisters if we understand the mystery given to Paul. When we understand Paul's distinctive apostleship and his sound doctrine from Christ, we are more likely to "walk in the Spirit" (Gal. 5:16) and "put ye on the Lord Jesus Christ, and make not provision for the flesh, to fulfil the lusts thereof" (13:14). Christ went to Israel in spite of their unbelief because that is what the Father wanted Him to do, and we should be willing to help those who are weak in Pauline truth (immature in sound doctrine) and have become <u>stuck under the law</u> because they follow Peter (and believe that the body of Christ began in Acts 2, instead of Acts 9). <u>The dispensation of grace and the body of Christ began when Christ saved Paul on the road to Damascus in Acts 9</u>. All of us brothers and sisters who are strong in the faith should be careful when helping those who are weak in sound doctrine. Edify or "build up" others in the word (do not tear them down over petty differences). Teach the rightly divided "word of his grace, which is able to build you up" (Acts 20:32). Try to help people who are ignorant and blind to the understanding that God began a new dispensation during Israel's partial national blindness (11:25) so all nations can be saved and live "<u>eternal in the heavens</u>" (2 Cor. 5:1).

**15:3-6 "For even Christ pleased not himself; but, as it is written, <u>The reproaches of them that reproached thee fell on me.</u>"** (Paul quotes Psa. 69:9). Christ bore the shame of those who shamed Him (Psa. 22:6-8). Christians are to follow the example of Christ, who did not live to please Himself (Phil. 2:5-8). So we should be able to bear a little <u>shame</u> from a weaker brother who may be resistant to sound doctrine because they don't understand it or those who criticize us. We should be willing to suffer affliction and reproach for the truth just as Christ did from those He came to save (John 1:11). We are to follow the example of Christ who did not live to please Himself. Notice how Paul points us to Jesus as our example when we know that Paul suffered a lot of reproach from the Jews and also from the Corinthian brethren. What Paul just quoted in Psa. 69:9 is for our learning. "<u>**For whatsoever things were written aforetime were written for our learning, that we through patience and comfort of the scriptures might have hope**</u>" (15:4). God's love, justice, grace, and mercy throughout the Bible comforts us and gives us hope. We can learn from all the Bible rightly divided. Paul also suffered reproach (1 Cor. 9:19-23). We should be willing to suffer reproach for the lost so they may be saved, and those weak in Pauline sound doctrine. "Yea, and all that will live godly in Christ Jesus shall suffer persecution" (2 Tim. 3:12). We gain spiritual comfort of the scriptures by experience. The Bible is spiritual nourishment from our Head "in whom are hid all treasures of wisdom and knowledge" (Col. 2:2-3). We must view all the Bible from a Pauline perspective. All the Bible is "for us," but not all of the Bible is "to" or "about us." I believe that God was killing two birds with one stone so to speak, and that He was sharing information with Israel that He knew the body of Christ could profit from. That is why Paul says that "All scripture . . . is profitable" (2 Tim. 3:16, 17). We will only get the profit out of the Bible that God has for us if we study it diligently rightly dividing. The God of patience provides consolation (comfort) as we in the body of Christ follow Paul (1 Cor. 11:1). We are to be likeminded with Christ willing to bear the reproach of others. We glorify the Father of our risen Lord Jesus Christ and are of one mind and one mouth when we follow what He said to us through Paul. We unite behind His apostle Paul. Receive each other and those weak in the faith (that mix Peter and Paul). They are weak for they are saved but unlearned in Pauline truth nevertheless God received them and us into the body.

**15:7-12 ¶** For this reason, we are to receive the weaker brother and try to help them come to Pauline truth as Christ has also received us to the glory of God. **Now I say that Jesus Christ was a minister of the circumcision for the truth of God, to confirm the promises made unto the fathers** (15:8; Deut. 9:5). Now Paul said that Christ was a minister to the Jews first (Rom. 1:16) when He was on earth in the previous dispensation so that Israel could save the Gentiles in prophecy. He quotes several Old Testament scriptures about Gentile salvation in prophecy in the future kingdom. Christ's earthly ministry to Israel confirmed the promises of eternal life and so on that God made unto Abraham, Isaac, and Jacob (his twelve sons became the twelve tribes). Christ came to Israel so that the nation of Israel could be saved and then be a "kingdom of priests" to save Gentiles in prophecy (Ex. 19:5, 6; Isa. 61:6). God intended to use His nation to bless all nations (Gen. 12:3) with the opportunity of salvation saying "in thy seed shall all the nations of the earth be blessed" (Gen. 22:18; Gal. 3:13-16). Christ let the woman of Canaan know that the Gentiles will be blessed after the overflow of Israel's fullness (Matt. 15:24-28). There is a parallel in the two programs because Gentiles can be saved in both, but the Gentiles in Israel's program will not be on the same level with Israel because the middle wall of partition will be up. So that the Gentiles might glorify God for His mercy "as it is written, For this cause I will confess to thee among the Gentiles, and sing unto thy name" (Psa. 18:49). Christ wants Israel to confess (declare) Him to the Gentiles in prophecy and sing to His name. Whenever Paul says "as it is written" that means he is quoting the Old Testament. Gentiles saved through Israel in prophecy should praise God. As they will, we should praise the Lord, give Him honor, and sing to Him. Just as the Gentiles in prophecy will rejoice when they are saved in the millennial kingdom we should rejoice now that we are saved. "And again, Praise the Lord, all ye Gentiles; and laud him, all ye people" (Psa. 117:1). "**And again, Esaias saith, There shall be a <u>root of Jesse,</u>** [King Jesus (Isa. 11:1)] **and <u>he that shall rise to reign over the Gentiles; in him shall the Gentiles trust</u>** [in the future kingdom]" (15:12; Isa. 11:10). Jesus Christ is the root (life giver) that shall come out of Jesse (David's seed-line) and rule over the Gentiles "in him shall the Gentiles trust." There is a pattern that progresses, the Gentiles hear the word (Psa. 18:49); Gentiles rejoice with the Jews (Deut. 32:43); All the Gentiles, praise God (Psa. 117:1); The Gentiles trust Christ and enjoy His millennial reign (Isa. 11:10). The Gentiles can believe in Messiah and join the Jews in prophecy, so allow the Jews to believe Paul's gospel and join with us Gentiles in mystery. <u>The Lord loves us, the body of Christ, just as much as He loves Israel.</u>

**15:13, 14** "<u>Now</u> **the <u>God of hope</u> fill you with all joy and peace in believing, that ye may <u>abound in hope, through the power of the Holy Ghost.</u> I myself also am persuaded of you, my brethren, that ye also are <u>full of goodness, filled with all knowledge,</u> able also to admonish one another**" (15:13, 14). Paul says "<u>now</u>" and switches to joy and peace from the "God of hope" in the present dispensation. We can be generous in sharing our knowledge because we abound in hope of the Rapture. God has always wanted to save the Gentiles in every dispensation. The wonderful thing is that <u>today Jews can be saved into the body of Christ</u> in God's time of salvation opportunity for the Gentiles by joining them. But <u>in the kingdom, God will give the Gentiles a 1,000-year opportunity to be saved in Israel's program.</u> Paul is persuaded that the believers in Rome understand the mystery. He knows these saints already knew that Christ wanted to save Gentiles in Israel's program and in His mystery program into the body of Christ. Daniel Webster's 1828 dictionary definition of "admonish" is "to warn, correct, notify of a fault; to reprove with mildness." It is best to correct someone who we notice has a wrong understanding, privately. Paul trusts that the Romans believers are full of goodness and can admonish each other with their knowledge of His word, but he still boldly wanted to be certain to establish them in the fundamental knowledge that he lays out in Romans. They know that Paul has a special commission to reach the Gentiles with the gospel and to share the mystery with all believers (apart from going through Israel's priests). <u>The churches Paul founded were busy making copies of the letters from him that were inspired by God and most likely had copies of all his letters (1 Tim. 3:15). There was no need for Paul to repeat what he said about being "caught up" or the resurrection in a "twinkling of an eye" because they had read that already</u> (1 Thess. 4:17; 1 Cor. 15:52).

**15:15, 16** "**Nevertheless, brethren, I have written the more boldly unto you in some sort, as putting you in mind, because of the grace that is given to me of God, That I should be the minister of Jesus Christ to the Gentiles, ministering the <u>gospel of God</u>, that <u>the offering up of the Gentiles might be acceptable, being <u>sanctified by the Holy Ghost</u>**" (15:15, 16). Nevertheless, Paul says he has written boldly to the believers in Rome and reminds them that God has made a <u>dispensational shift from Israel to the Gentiles</u>. Paul describes the "grace" that was given him by God in 15:16, he was appointed by Christ to be His minister to <u>purify</u> the Gentiles (Acts 26:16-18). <u>Paul did not take that office by himself, God chose to give Paul that authority</u> (Acts 9:15). Christ enabled Paul who was a blasphemer of the Holy Ghost (1 Tim. 1:12, 13) by joining in the stoning of Stephen, to nevertheless, be His minister. Christ said blasphemy of the Holy Ghost would "not be forgiven him, neither in this world, neither in the world to come" (Matt. 12:31, 32). Therefore, Paul could only be forgiven in the new dispensation God inserted. Paul wants to be proud of the Gentile believers in mystery when Christ presents us to the Father (1 Thess. 3:13). <u>What an apostle's heart he had</u>! It will be a privilege for all of us to meet him. The "gospel of God" appears 7 times in the King James Bible, 6 in Paul's writings, and once in Peter's (1 Peter 4:17). <u>The gospel of God is the basic prophesied information of Christ's death, burial, and resurrection for sins</u>. Both Peter and Paul preached the basic gospel of the Redeemer for both groups. But Peter emphasized the <u>gospel of the kingdom</u> and Paul the <u>gospel of Christ</u>. Peter said that Christ was the King of the Jews to sit on the throne in the coming kingdom. <u>Paul preached Christ crucified and risen for our justification by faith</u> (4:24, 25). The <u>gospel of Christ</u> is clear in 1 Corinthians 15:3, 4. So what is the difference between Paul's gospel and Peter's? Paul said Christ died for <u>OUR</u> SINS (Jews and Gentiles in mystery) apart from Israel. Paul never said that the body of Christ would live in a kingdom on earth but in heavenly places (Eph. 2:6, 2 Cor. 5:1). Gospel means "good news." There is more than one gospel in the Bible but there is only one that saves today, Paul's. <u>Paul has the authority to instruct the body of Christ on how to live in mystery so that the body of Christ will be acceptable to God being sanctified (set apart for service) by the Holy Ghost. Today, Christ is manifested to the world through the believer</u> (1 Tim. 3:16).

**15:17-23** Paul could glory in the authority Christ gave him. He was made His minister in those things that pertain to God. Paul said that since he has received this apostleship therefore he concentrates on the commission and authority Christ gave him. Paul said he does not dare to speak of any of those things which Christ has not worked "by me" to make the Gentiles obedient (believe and obey) by <u>word and deed</u> by what Christ gave Paul to say and do. Christ empowered Paul to do the supernatural signs of an apostle (2 Cor. 12:12), it was the "power of the Spirit of

God" (15:19) working in Paul. We have that same Spirit in us even if signs have ceased. That power helped Paul fully preach the gospel of Christ to the Gentiles from Jerusalem round about to Illyricum. After the uproar in Ephesus (which was a mob that chanted for two hours and basically wanted to tear Paul apart) Paul went to Macedonia, then to Illyricum, and then down to Corinth. After salvation, we can also speak the truth and do good works as we serve God just like our "pattern" Paul (1 Tim. 1:16). Paul is our pattern, so we should copy what he does. "Those things, which ye have both learned, and received, and heard, and seen in me, do and the God of peace shall be with you" (Phil. 4:9). In order to live a godly life, we must have the sound doctrine found in Paul's epistles built up in our inner man. When we do that we have peace and are in God's will (1 Tim. 2:4).

**15:20-23** Paul said, I endeavor to preach the gospel, not where others have preached Him, so I would not build on another man's foundation (Peter's message). Paul broke up new ground. **"But as it is written, To whom he was not spoken of, they shall see: and they that have not heard shall understand"** (Paul quotes Isa. 52:15). Paul quotes a trans-dispensational verse. God wants people to hear about Him in every dispensation. Christ is the foundation for both prophecy and mystery. Paul was commissioned to preach to those heathen (unsaved Jews and Gentiles) who had not heard about a chance for salvation, while Peter and his group ministered to the saved Jews, the circumcision who had believed the gospel of the kingdom (Gal. 2:9). This is the way Paul did not build on Peter's foundation (message). In prophecy, the Jews needed to be saved first so they could be priests to the Gentiles in the kingdom (Acts 11:19). Christ sent Paul to preach to those who had not seen or heard the gospel (Acts 26:16-18). Christ spoke to Paul by revelation, and the Holy Spirit also used the Old Testament scriptures. For the cause of preaching to those who had not heard, Paul had been hindered from coming to them in Rome. Paul had been busy preaching to the heathen. But now Paul does not have a place left to preach in those parts. Please note that Paul decided to visit Rome after he witnessed the marvelous transformation of the Ephesians. Due to the doctrine working in them they voluntarily decided to burn their many costly occult books (Acts 19:21). He made this decision before he was forced to leave Ephesus because of the uproar caused by the silversmiths (Acts 19:29-32, 40). Having covered the other ground preaching the gospel so everyone had heard from Jerusalem to Illyricum, Paul has had a great desire for many years to come to them. He plans to see them on his way to Spain, but first, he is going to Jerusalem to deliver some money that the Macedonians and the Corinthians, and the neighboring Achia (southern Greece) had collected. Paul wrote Romans just before leaving to go to Jerusalem with two delegates from each contributing region including Galatia (Acts 20:3-6). Luke joined the party in Philippi.

**15:24-29** Whenever he does take his journey into Spain, he will come to visit them, enjoy their company, and be brought on his way by them. But for now, he will soon be on his way to Jerusalem to bring some money to the poor saints, Peter's group. The little flock had sold everything as Christ had told them to do so since they were supposed to be heading into "Jacob's trouble" (Jer. 30:7; Luke 12:32, 33; Acts 4:34, 35). They were anticipating going into the Tribulation and would not be able to buy or sell because they would not take the "mark of the beast" (Rev. 13:18; 16:2). The Gentiles in Macedonia and Achaia had made "**a certain contribution for the poor saints which are at Jerusalem**" (15:26). The Gentiles are in their debt because they have been made partakers of their "spiritual things" (His Spirit, adoptions as sons, and hope of eternal life). Spiritually the little flock saints are "in Christ" and "Christ is in them" (John 17:26; Gal. 1:22). Now Christ is in us and we are in Him (Col. 1:27; Rom. 12:5). Peter and the remnant have been placed on hold, their program has been postponed (Acts 15:14-16; Gal. 2:7-9). The Gentiles' "**duty is also to minister unto them in carnal things** [material things]" (15:27) since God has postponed Israel's program and is giving the Gentiles an opportunity to believe directly on what Christ has done apart from going through Israel. Paul is also bringing the money gift for the purpose of having the little flock's good will and blessing so that there would be no strife between the two groups of believers. The Christians would be edified being able to do their duty and give, while the saints in Jerusalem would experience Christian love in action. After Paul had finished the task and the saints at Jerusalem had securely received the gift of money, Paul plans to swing by and visit them on his way to Spain. Paul wants churches established in all the major strategic cities. Somehow Christ must have communicated to Paul that he would have the full revelation of the mystery by the time he arrived in Rome (even if he had not written everything down yet). "**And I am sure that, when I come unto you, I shall come in the fulness of the blessing of the gospel of Christ** (15:29)." Paul would be able to share this further revelation with the saints at Rome when he arrived.

**15:30-33** Paul kindly asks them for the Lord Jesus Christ's sake and for the love of the Spirit, to help him by striving together with him in "**prayer to God for me.**" Prayer is work because the flesh does not want to do it. Paul believed in the power of prayer. He asked for specific prayer regarding three things: (1) him to be delivered from those who do not believe in Judaea, (2) that the gift will be accepted by the saints, and (3) that he may come to them in Rome with joy by the will of God, and be refreshed with them. He prays that the God of peace would be with them and closes the main portion of the letter. Were Paul's prayers answered? Yes! Paul arrived alive in Rome after the gift was accepted (Acts 21:15-17, 28:16) and he had more revelation.

**Romans Chapter 16 Salutations and benediction as to the Mystery**

**Romans 16:1-6** Paul commends Phebe, a saint that carried the letter to Rome, unto them. She served in a Pauline church at Cenchrea, a seaport near Corinth. He asks, please receive her in the Lord in the gracious manner that becomes saints and help her in every possible way, for she has been a helper of many including myself. Paul then greets many of the saints with personal expressions of love. Greet Priscilla and Aquila, my helpers in Christ Jesus (they had moved back to Rome). Who have for my life laid down their own necks. Why does Paul mention Priscilla first? Perhaps in the uproar (Acts 19:40) Priscilla may have been braver or she may have been stronger in the doctrine. Paul thanks them publically on the behalf of the Gentiles. Without Paul, the Gentile churches would have no further revelation from Jesus for His heavenly group. Likewise greet the church that is in their home. They had a house church. Paul mentions three or more house churches in this letter.

**16:7-16** Salute Andronicus and Junia, my kinsmen, and my fellowprisoners, who are respected by the 12 apostles. When Paul talks about <u>Andronicus and Junia</u> he makes it clear that they were "**in Christ**" (or saved) before him (16:7). They were saved by the preaching of the little flock; this is how they were "in Christ" before Paul. Since we know that Paul is the first one in the body of Christ (1 Tim. 1:16). What was the gospel that they had trusted? The gospel of the kingdom. They repented (changed their minds) and believed that Jesus Christ was the King of the Jews and were baptized with water and the Holy Ghost (Acts 2:38). They met Paul in prison (perhaps in Philippi, Acts 16:25). <u>Christ told Peter and the little flock that they will be in Him and He will be in them</u> (John 14:20, 17:23). However, those saints realized that God had changed dispensations and had begun working through a new apostle, Paul. They wanted to be part of what God is doing now so they joined Paul. Barnabas and Silas are examples of other "little flock" saints who also helped Paul. Paul mentions that his face for a while was unknown to the "churches of Judaea which were <u>in Christ</u>" (Gal. 1:22). Everyone who is saved is "in Christ" and not in Adam. We have so "much more" in Christ because we have the gift of His righteousness (5:17). In the fullness of times, God will gather everyone who is "in Christ" into the new <u>heaven</u> and the new <u>earth</u> (Eph. 1:10). Paul greets Amplias my beloved in the Lord. Possibly another house church. Salute Urbane, our helper in Christ, Stachys my beloved. Salute Herodion my kinsman, either a Jew or a relative of Paul. Greet them that be of the household of Narcissus, which are in the Lord (possibly another house church). Salute Tryphena and Tryphosa, <u>who labour in the Lord</u>. These women helped others to be saved and to come to the knowledge of the truth of sound doctrine getting the gospel out. <u>Women are to be faithful to share what they have learned about Pauline truth just like men are.</u>

**16:17-20 ¶** "Now I beseech you, brethren, <u>mark</u> them which cause divisions and offences <u>contrary to the doctrine which ye have learned</u>; <u>and avoid them.</u> Paul implores the believers to mark (identify, name) those who cause division and offences (cause believers to be separated from the truth by <u>false doctrine</u> and do wrong things). "Avoid them" do not listen to those who are teaching contrary to what Paul taught in this or other letters (for example <u>those who believe that the body of Christ began in Acts 2</u>). Most of these pastors preach Acts 2 out of <u>ignorance</u>, they just don't know any better. We must remember that we were like them. They are those who <u>do not serve the Lord Jesus Christ</u>. These teachers do not submit to the fact that Christ made Paul "the apostle of the Gentiles" (11:13) and that his letters (Romans to Philemon) is Christ's doctrine to the body of Christ during the dispensation of grace, not Matthew, Mark, Luke, and John. **"For they that are such <u>serve not our Lord Jesus Christ, but their <u>own belly</u>; and <u>by good words and fair speeches deceive the hearts of the simple</u>.**" (16:17, 18) <u>Unless the ministry is Pauline they are NOT serving Christ</u> (2 Cor. 11:13-15). They just want to promote themselves and their mixed-up beliefs. They do not know the truth and they care more about money to feed themselves rather than feeding others spiritual truth. They may sound eloquent and their spiritualizing of God's word and cute stories may sound like they are saying something of value, but they are not following Paul (1 Cor. 14:37). <u>The so called church fathers turned their backs to apostle Paul and steered people away from the truth of the mystery Christ revealed to Paul for us in the body of Christ. Satan has always been against what God is doing (1 Tim. 2:4) and is busy blinding the minds of people</u> (2 Cor. 4:3, 4). They deceive people who are not knowledgeable in the word of God to believe anything they hear without checking it out with the final authority, the King James Bible. They are easily persuaded to follow them. One pastor wants people to "have their best life now" without concern for suffering for the sake of the truth so that we may serve Christ in responsible job positions in eternity. Paul is glad for their sakes to hear that the believers in Rome are well known outside Rome for their faithfulness to follow Paul's sound doctrine (1:8). But Paul wants them to be wise unto that which is good (Paul's sound doctrine), and <u>simple concerning evil (false doctrine)</u>. Focus on truth, not error. Just like Christ, we can have faith in God's plan. God has told us to live by allowing Christ to live through us (12:1, 2). "Christ liveth in me" (Gal. 2:20). So now we live by the faith of the Son of God, offering our bodies as a living sacrifice. **"And <u>the God of peace shall bruise Satan under your feet shortly</u>**" (16:20). <u>Paul expects Christ to reveal the entire mystery to him soon (15:29). With Christ's Spirit living through us using His doctrine we bruise Satan and his false ministers under our feet. Satan and his workers cannot stand Paul's powerful truth.</u> It is in Paul's epistles that Christ's triumph over him is made known (Col. 2:15). But Satan does what he can <u>to conceal Pauline truth</u>. When believers are strong in the truth with Christ working through them laboring to get the message out Satan is bruised. However, when Satan and his angels are cast out and we replace them, then Satan will be truly bruised under out feet (Rev. 12:7-9).

**16:21-24** ¶ Some brothers with Paul (Timotheus his fellow worker, Lucius, Jason, and Sosipater his kinsman) and the secretary or amanuensis who wrote down the dictated letter, Tertius, say hello. Paul only wrote Galatians with his own hand (Gal. 6:11). Gaius my host, and the whole church (at Corinth) salute you (probably the Gaius in 1 Cor. 1:14). Erastus the chamberlain or City Treasurer in Corinth (2 Tim. 4:20) and Quartus a brother says hello.

**16:25-27** ¶ **"Now to him that is of power to stablish you according to my gospel,"** Paul ends with a benediction to God. God can stablish the believer by three things: (1) "My gospel," (2) "The preaching of Jesus Christ, according to the revelation of the mystery," and (3) "By the scriptures and the prophets" meaning all scripture, both the Old and New Testament, outside Paul's epistles rightly divided (as the scriptures relate from a Pauline perspective). Christ's living Spirit in us has the power to use His living word in us because we are His workmanship (Eph. 2:10). "My gospel" is the imputed righteousness of Christ, justification by faith. When we believe Paul's gospel a transaction occurs, God imputes our sins on Christ and imputes the Son's righteousness (His life, Spirit) to us (3:22-26, 4:22-25, 5:1; 1 Cor. 15:3, 4; 2 Cor. 5:21). When we have the righteousness of Christ God declares us perfectly righteous and justified so we can then come before the Holy Father without being obliterated. We have been translated out of Adam into Christ and out of Satan's kingdom into the kingdom of His dear Son (1 Cor. 15:22; Col. 1:13, 14). Paul calls it "my gospel" to distinguish it from the gospel of the kingdom given to the twelve. "My gospel" is the "gospel of Christ" and the "gospel of grace," and the audience Paul preached to is the uncircumcision, the Gentiles. Paul's gospel is the only gospel that saves today. Paul is the only apostle of the Gentiles (11:13). He says that Christ died for OUR SINS (the Gentiles in mystery). Paul makes it clear Christ died to be a "ransom for all" (1 Tim. 2:6). In this age, anyone can be saved by believing what Christ has accomplished for him.

**"and the preaching of Jesus Christ, according to the revelation of the mystery, which was kept secret since the world began, But now is made manifest,"** God has now revealed the mystery through Paul (Eph. 3:1-9). Paul calls his doctrine the "mystery" because it was kept secret until it was revealed to him. Jesus Christ Himself revealed the mystery to Paul. He did not receive it from another man such as Peter, and he didn't need another man to teach him (Gal. 1:1, 11, 12). The mystery revelation was not known until Christ first revealed it to Paul in Acts 9.

He was first (1 Tim. 1:16). The mystery was unsearchable (Eph. 3:8.) No creature was as surprised as Satan when Christ returned after a year in heaven and saved His worst enemy on the road to Damascus. "What?" Satan thought, "that is not what the scriptures say? That is un-prophesied! That was not what was supposed to happen next! Where is God's wrath on His people?" God defeated Satan by keeping a secret. The main mystery is the formation of the body of Christ during the dispensation of grace to live in heaven. Compare this to what Peter says in Acts 3:19-21. The mystery is the entire body of doctrine given to Paul by revelation from the risen, ascended, glorified Lord Jesus Christ (Romans to Philemon).

**"and by the scriptures of the prophets,"** The rest of the Bible, (prophecy), the scriptures outside of Paul's writings. Both the Old Testament and New Testament scriptures (rightly divided). To be more clear Genesis to Acts 9 and Hebrews to Revelation are prophecy. **"according to the commandment of the everlasting God, made known to all nations for the obedience of faith:"** God has commanded that all nations believe the gospel that He made known to Paul, and then come to the knowledge of the truth (1 Tim. 2:4). Paul progressively received the revelation that God is now forming the body of Christ, (the one new man, Eph. 2:15) during the dispensation of grace, to reign with Christ in the heavenly places. So all people can believe the sound doctrine Christ gave us through Paul. **"To God only wise, be glory through Jesus Christ for ever. Amen."** God alone is wise. It was Satan that "weakened the nations" (Isa. 14:12). But God kept a secret from Satan and caught him in His own craftiness (1 Cor. 3:19). "Howbeit we speak wisdom among them that are perfect: yet not the wisdom of this world, nor of the princes of this world, that come to nought: But we speak the wisdom of God in a mystery, even the hidden wisdom, which God ordained before the world unto our glory: Which none of the princes of this world knew: for had they known it, they would not have crucified the Lord of glory" (1 Cor. 2:6-8). In His wisdom, God kept the mystery formation of the body of Christ a secret from Satan because if he knew he would lose the heavenly places along with the earth he would not have crucified the Lord of glory. It was the cross of Christ, the Son's death for mankind's sins and resurrection that redeemed both groups of believers who will live in heaven and earth. It was God's Plan to save us and glorify His Son in both spheres which was determined by the Godhead before the foundation of the world (Acts 2:23; Eph. 1:9, 10; 1 Peter 1:18-20). God is wise and we can trust the Father and the Son to rule wisely. Paul gives God all the glory through Jesus Christ and so should we because He has done everything that was necessary to save us. Amen.

We have a closer walk with Him when we understand His word more precisely.

# Appendix

## One Year Extension of Mercy for Israel

Although the prophetic clock according to Daniel's timeline stopped at the cross, Israel received a bonus year of mercy from God. In addition to asking the Father to forgive them because of their ignorance while on the cross, <u>Jesus had also pleaded with the Father to give His people one more year</u> to repent and receive Him as their Messiah. Jesus said, "A certain *man* [God the Father] had a fig tree planted in his vineyard; and he came and sought fruit [faith] thereon, and found none. Then said he [God the Father] **unto the dresser of his vineyard** [God the Son], **Behold, these three years I come seeking fruit on this fig tree** [Israel], **and find none: cut it down; why cumbereth it the ground? And he** [the Son] **answering said unto him, Lord,** <u>let it alone this year also</u> [give Israel one more year], **till I shall dig about it, and dung** [fertilize by the power of the Holy Ghost] *it*: **And if it bear fruit,** *well*: **and if not,** *then* **after that thou shalt** <u>cut it down</u> [<u>cut off</u> Israel for a season]" **(Luke 13:6-9).**

But Peter and the disciples of Christ, the little remnant (the little flock) did have faith in Him, so <u>the kingdom was taken from the unbelieving nation of Israel and given to the remnant of believing Israel.</u> "**Therefore say I** [Jesus] **unto you** [the religious leaders of the nation of Israel], **The kingdom of God shall be taken from you, and given to a nation** [the little flock] **bringing forth the fruits** [faith] **thereof**" (Matt. 21:43).

The little flock (believing remnant) received the kingdom. "**Fear not**<u>, little flock</u>**; for it is your Father's good pleasure** <u>to give you the kingdom</u>" (Luke 12:32). When Peter asked Jesus what he would receive for his faithfulness Jesus answered "Verily I say unto you, That <u>ye which have followed me, in the regeneration</u> [when the Earth is regenerated in the millennium] <u>when the Son of man shall sit in the throne of his glory, ye</u> [the twelve Apostles] <u>also shall sit upon twelve thrones, judging the twelve tribes of Israel</u>" (Matthew 19:28).

Three times a year Israel was to keep a feast to the LORD. These feasts are a picture of God's plan to redeem them. Christ has already fulfilled Passover, Unleavened Bread, and Firstfruits (held in Abib, the first month). The next, Pentecost (50 days later) was fulfilled in Acts 2. The Feast of Trumpets, Day of Atonement, and Feast of Tabernacles (in the 7<sup>th</sup> month) will be fulfilled when Israel is gathered into their land, the nation is forgiven, and Messiah rules and lives with them. <u>The final feasts, as we have learned, have been postponed.</u>

## About the Author

She was saved in 1990. She became, not only a King James Bible user, but a King James Bible believer in 2014. She has more than twenty-five years of experience teaching the Bible, eighteen of those years were with the AWANA clubs where she earned her Citation Award for Bible memorization. In 2015, she was introduced to Pauline dispensational truth by watching Les Feldick on YouTube. After learning the basics of "rightly dividing the word of truth" (2 Timothy 2:15), she learned more from the Bible and Richard Jordan and his Grace School of the Bible. A retired nurse midwife, she has devoted the rest of her life "to make all men see what is the fellowship of the mystery" (Eph. 3:9). She teaches a Bible study in her home which is available on Facebook and YouTube (mariannemanley.com). Her joy after understanding the Bible better led her to edify the body of Christ by writing **God's Secret** in 2017. **Romans: A Concise Commentary, First Corinthians: A Commentary, Second Corinthians: A Commentary, Galatians: A Commentary, Treasure Hunt Volume I** (Romans to Galatians), **Ephesians A Commentary, Philippians, Colossians, Philemon Commentary, Treasure Hunt Volume II** (Paul's Prison Epistles), **Why was the Earth without Form, Void, and Dark?**, **Just as God Said** for children, **The Certainty of the Pre-Tribulation Rapture** (First and Second Thessalonians Commentary), **Paul's Pastoral Epistles** (First and Second Timothy, Titus, and Philemon Commentary), **Treasure Hunt Volume III** (Paul's T Books), **Acts of the Apostles Commentary Part 1, 2, 3, Missed the Rapture? Read this Commentary on Hebrew!** and **How to be Saved Made Simple**, **Why the King James Bible is the Holy Bible**, and the **Rightly Dividing Study Guides**. Many people have all her books!

**Other Books by Marianne Manley**

*God's Secret  A Primer with Pictures for How to Rightly Divide the Word of Truth* (on Amazon.com in **Black and White Edition**, and in Spanish *El Secreto de Dios*).

*Why the King James Bible is the Holy Bible*
*Rightly Dividing COLOSSIANS and PHILEMON Study Guide*
*Rightly Dividing PHILIPPIANS Study Guide*
*Rightly Dividing EPHISIANS Study Guide*
*Rightly Dividing GALATIANS Study Guide*
*Rightly Dividing SECOND CORINTHIANS Study Guide*
*Rightly Dividing FIRST CORINTHIANS Study Guide*
*Rightly Dividing ROMANS Study Guide*
*Romans: A Concise Commentary* (also in a Black and White Edition)
*First Corinthians: A Commentary*
*Second Corinthians: A Commentary*
*Galatians: A Commentary*
*Ephesians A Commentary*
*Philippians, Colossians, Philemon Commentary*
*The Certainty of the Pre-Tribulation Rapture* (First and Second Thessalonians)
*Paul's Pastoral Epistles* (Timothy Letters, Titus, and Philemon Commentary)
*Treasure Hunt Volume I* (Commentary only Romans to Galatians)
*Treasure Hunt Volume II* (Commentary only on Paul's Prison Epistles)
*Treasure Hunt Volume III* (Commentary on Paul's T Books)

*Why was the Earth without Form, Void, and Dark?*
*Just as God Said*
*Acts of the Apostles Commentary Part One, Two, Three*
*Missed the Rapture? Read this Commentary on Hebrews!*
*How to be Saved Made Simple* (This booklet is perfect for our lost loved ones.)
*Could God Have a 7,000 Year Plan for Mankind?* (also in Black and White and
*AD 34 The Year Jesus Died for All* (same content as Could God, in 9x6 size)

The author may be contacted by e-mail at mariannemanley@sbcglobal.net
Please visit her website: www.mariannemanley.com (free .pdf files)
Follow her on Facebook at facebook.com/marianne.manley.7 and God's
Secret Facebook Page at facebook.com/GodsSecretAPrimerwithPictures
Find her on YouTube (Just type in her name and find her teaching the Bible, a-chapter-at-a-time) or on Salvation, Rightly Dividing, and the Rapture her YouTube channel or Truth Be Told, or call (858) 273-2049.

Made in United States
North Haven, CT
29 November 2023

44754602R00041